HISPANIC MEDIA
Impact and Influence

HISPANIC MEDIA

Impact and Influence

*By Ana Veciana-Suarez
With a Foreword by Manuel Galvan*

This book was made possible by funding from

(**the media institute**)
Washington, D.C.

HISPANIC MEDIA: IMPACT AND INFLUENCE

Copyright © 1990 The Media Institute

All rights reserved. No part of this publication may be reproduced or transmitted in any form without permission in writing from the publisher.

First printing January 1990.

Published by The Media Institute, Washington, D.C.

Printed in the United States of America.

ISBN: 0-937790-41-9

Library of Congress Catalog Card Number: 89-63531

Table of Contents

Foreword
    Manuel Galvan, Chicago Tribune   vii

Introduction   1

I.   Hispanic Media Overview   5

II.   The Hispanic Market   11

III.   The National Agenda   17

IV.   Los Angeles   29

V.   New York   37

VI.   Miami   47

VII.   San Antonio   55

VIII.   Chicago   63

IX.   The Future   73

Notes   79

Foreword

Just as English-language media cannot be generalized, neither can Spanish-language newspapers, radio stations, and television networks be lumped together as one conglomerate with a single mind or purpose. Each has its own character, complete with virtues, faults, and a unique market.

Collectively, however, there exists an image of the Hispanic media, a perception, if you will. It is an image of a rapidly growing Hispanic population with an often ill-prepared Spanish-language media industry struggling to keep up with the growth.

There are exceptions, of course. The Spanish-language networks frequently give better coverage of Latin America than do the mainstream giants. Dozens of radio stations are crucial to their listeners' understanding of their communities, and a handful of newspapers do their best to inform, entertain, and make money.

There is also a very real difference in the way Spanish-language journalism is practiced. In many ways, Hispanic media are behind their counterparts by several decades, not so much in technology as in ethics and professionalism.

If I had to choose one word to describe the Spanish-language media's biggest obstacle to success it would be "credibility."

For starters, there is the matter of Hispanic media being an advocacy press. Many would argue there is no such thing as objectivity in media because choices are made in the selection of news and how it is played. Just as many, though, would acknowledge that the media should always strive to be fair and impartial.

That is not the case in an advocacy press, which sees a duty to defend and argue a "cause." In the case of the Latino media, this means advocacy for Hispanics. There is nothing wrong with this; but to the non-involved reader or listener this often becomes a matter of "us and them."

In 1983 when the late Harold Washington won the Democratic mayoral primary, tantamount in Chicago to winning the City Hall post, the <u>Chicago Daily Defender</u>, a black advocacy newspaper, ran the following headline: "We won."

An advocacy press is given less ranking than mainstream media. In addition, Spanish-language media are often seen as coloring the issues in favor of Hispanics, despite the reality of the situation.

Even within the Spanish media there are warring causes. Charges are flying about networks becoming "Cubanized" because of the disproportionate number of Cubans in top jobs.

In Chicago, where the diverse Hispanic community mirrors that of the United States, there are "Puerto Rican" newspapers and "Mexican" newspapers which often take opposite sides when more of one group is being hired in City Hall. There are also politically left newspapers and their counterparts to the right. When Mayor Washington was honored at a community forum together with the Nicaraguan minister of culture, a conservative Spanish newspaper ran a banner headline in red, reading: "The mayor, a communist."

When a media outlet is so skewed, readers beyond those cheering and denouncing along with it have little faith in the product. Ironically, this is where the United States media were in the 19th century when newspapers were formed along political party lines, and gave themselves names like the "Republican" and the "Democrat."

Spanish-language newspapers, mainly the weeklies, also damage their credibility by lying about their circulation figures to boost their status and advertising.

When major advertisers take the time to investigate circulation claims by talking to people and visiting stores, they sometimes find the figures false and take their business elsewhere. Unfortunately, too often they assume "Spanish newspapers are all like that." Fortunately, there is the National Association of Hispanic Publications, which, to help increase credibility, requires that the circulation figures of its members be audited.

There is also the matter of management at Spanish-language outlets. In some cases, the owners and publishers ran newspapers in Latin American countries before coming to the United States. Their practice of journalism is one of boosterism, often at the cost of accuracy.

One newspaper publisher got started in Chicago several years ago because he was promoting boxing matches and no one covered them to his satisfaction.

The owners also show very little concern for conflict-of-interest matters. When a reporter at a Spanish-language TV station in Chicago was prepared to run a story exposing a beauty school for taking students' money and federal funding in return for neither education nor placement, the station manager killed the story because the beauty school was a regular advertiser.

Newspapers regularly engage in a form of bartering with their advertisers. A travel agency gives a free trip and the paper runs a free ad. A restaurant provides free meals and the eatery gets a free ad and, perhaps, a good review. The result: The value of the product and the profession is cheapened and credibility again suffers.

Reporters are often at a disadvantage in career opportunities. While the pay is not great for starting newspaper reporters in the mainstream -- $14,000 annually -- it is even less for those at Spanish-language outlets. In addition, many of these outlets cannot afford health benefits for their entire staff. They sometimes circumvent this by keeping a reporter on part-time status, which, in turn, forces the reporter to take a supplemental job, which increases the potential for a conflict of interest.

Starting reporters at mainstream outlets frequently have a journalism degree. This is not often the case in the Spanish media. If a reporter has a degree and is bilingual, he or she will usually apply to the mainstream media first. In addition, because editors and managers are usually not seasoned professionals, the starting Spanish reporter gets very little training to help improve and advance in his or her career.

Because the outlets seem to have few resources, their backup support -- a library, research staff, graphics department -- is weak. Often, they are under deadline pressure and report stories without much more than quotes. It is not uncommon for press releases to be reprinted verbatim.

These are some of the problems Ana Veciana-Suarez addresses in this book. The reader will find that this volume is much more than a compilation of vital information about Spanish-language media outlets in the major Hispanic markets, although it is certainly that. Likewise, the reader will find it more than a chronicle of this country's evolving Hispanic population, its demographic characteristics, and political trends, although it is that too.

The importance of this book, I believe, lies in the fact that it gives us a concise picture of how Spanish-language outlets perceive their performance -- and thus their impact and influence -- within their communities. Perhaps of greater importance, this book gives us an extremely candid look at how community leaders perceive the effectiveness of these media. The perceptions of these leaders are often very different, and more critical, than those of the media representatives.

The book is based on the many interviews Ana conducted in five major Hispanic markets. As an experienced reporter, Ana Veciana-Suarez has given us a fine piece of reporting. In fact, a major strength of this book is the fact that it is a "hands on," first-person account of Hispanic media as they exist today, told by someone who has examined them at close range.

As an observer and analyst of Hispanic culture, Ana adds to her reporting the benefit of her insights into what current developments mean, and what they bode for the future of U.S. Hispanic media. The result is a book which is practical without being pedestrian, insightful without being lost in abstraction. As the pages herein note, Spanish-language media have a responsibility not only to inform their audiences about local, national, and international topics, but to do so in the most responsible and professional manner. Those outlets which can successfully bridge the "credibility gap" face bright prospects for increased impact and influence. Those which cannot will never achieve influence, if indeed they survive at all. I don't think Ana will disagee when I say that major gains have been made, but the journey is far from over.

Manuel Galvan
Chicago, Illinois
November 1989

Manuel Galvan is a member of the editorial board of the <u>Chicago Tribune</u>. He is a past president and founding member of The National Association of Hispanic Journalists, and authored <u>The World Book Encyclopedia</u> entry on Hispanics.

Introduction

When The Media Institute and I began talking about a followup to our first book on Hispanic media, we toyed with different ideas before arriving at the concept for this book. Hispanic Media: Impact and Influence was conceived as a work that would look at the effects of Spanish-language mass media on society. Certainly, the way newspapers, radio, and television influence our thoughts and actions, our beliefs and mores, is the most important aspect of communication in any language.

Since earliest times we have shaped and been shaped by the media available to us, be those clay tablets, newspapers, or broadcast stations. How then have the Spanish-language media of the United States in the last decades of this century shaped us? That is the question I hope to answer.

Methodology

By no means is this book a scientific survey. Nor are the conclusions cited here intended to be regarded as empirical data. Rather, Hispanic Media: Impact and Influence is based almost exclusively on interviews and personal observations. Unlike the growing academic literature in this field, it is more of a hands-on, anecdotal approach to the subject. Although the sources for the book provided a wide range of opinion -- sometimes agreeing, sometimes not -- in no way are their opinions a comprehensive listing. However, this said, I believe the method of personal interviews with local leaders provides a relatively accurate picture of a community's perception of its Spanish-language media. These perceptions, in turn, reflect the ability of media to influence, in one way or another, the opinions of the opinion molders themselves.

The Media Institute and I selected these opinion molders with the help of journalists, university political science departments, and Spanish-language media owners. Our goal was to obtain as broad a spectrum of political ideas and social experience as possible in order to reflect the greatest diversity of opinion. We knew, of course, that each of these local leaders would have his or her own ax to grind; therefore, while opinions of these leaders are not necessarily "objective," they do reflect the reality of perceptions toward Spanish-language media.

In each of the cities I visited, I interviewed elected and appointed officials at various levels of government, grassroots activists, a businessman (usually identified by the local Hispanic chamber of commerce), and a university professor who had studied the Spanish media in his or her area. In some cases, when an organization was identified as a leading force within the community -- the Mexican-American Legal Defense and Educational Fund (MALDEF), for instance, or Chicago's Latino Institute -- I met either with the director or the person who regularly deals with the media, such as the director of communications. When possible, I also interviewed media directors or heads of advertising agencies. Because of time, economic, and space factors, I could not interview everyone identified by my sources as leaders. However, the basis for selection was an interviewee's extensive use of the media -- usually both as a consumer and as a newsmaker. Thus, I found that almost everyone I spoke to had used Spanish-language media as part of his or her daily information-gathering for many years. They had also used newspapers and broadcast outlets in their areas to publicize events or promote ideas.

In addition, when I found groups such as the Latino Committee on the Media in Chicago or the Hispanic Media Coalition in Los Angeles, I interviewed their members to find out what self-appointed critics, including ex-journalists, thought of their local press and broadcast outlets. In some cases, these sources are quoted in the book. Others served to provide a variety of background information and excellent leads.

I visited five cities -- Los Angeles, New York, Miami, San Antonio, and Chicago. The first four are the country's top Hispanic markets in that order. Chicago is the sixth-largest Hispanic market. I did not write about San Francisco, the fifth largest, because The Media Institute and I felt California was well represented by Los Angeles. But to omit Chicago, the top Hispanic market in the Midwest, would have been a disservice.

Defining the Terms

Though explained in more detail in Chapter 3, two important terms should be defined at the outset. **Power**, the ability to do or create something, is used interchangeably with _influence_ throughout these pages. Influence, as cited here, has two components: internal and external. Internal influence is the ability of an outlet to cause change within the community alone; it can often be measured by the respect and reputation enjoyed by the outlet within its own area. External influence, on the other hand, is the ability of this outlet to articulate the concerns of its Hispanic community to a wider Anglo audience, particularly the political powers. In each city, the reader will find that external influence is often much more difficult to determine. And while almost all outlets have some type of internal influence, few have the power to influence a larger universe.

Influence, or power, can be expressed in many forms: political, social, economic, cultural. Sometimes these influences are interrelated; sometimes they cannot be measured. For this book and in my interviews, I defined power as the ability to influence -- and bring about change -- by meeting certain criteria. These criteria included an outlet's ability to:

* Influence policy makers and opinion molders.
* Serve as a conduit between the audience and the powers that be.
* Mobilize a community.
* Change attitudes and values.
* Legitimize unknown grassroots movements and emerging leaders.

The interviewees were repeatedly asked for specific examples that demonstrated a newspaper's or station's ability to bring about change. Their power was measured by the end result. In other words, how successful was an outlet in mobilizing a community, legitimizing an emerging leader, influencing a government official?

What I found, not surprisingly, was that Spanish-language media wielded their power in many of the same ways as did their English-language counterparts. They also faced many of the same problems and made some of the same mistakes. These comparisons are noted briefly throughout the book.

The Role of Media

Finally, a word on two assumptions that are sure to garner some controversy. I state, in several sections, that it is better for Hispanics to own their own media outlets. I believe this for several reasons and found that, by and large, most of the people I interviewed agreed. The first, and probably most important reason, is that ownership provides control: Control of what is printed or aired, and what is not. Control of how resources are used and the budget managed. Control of the money that is earned in the normal course of an outlet's operation. This control translates into power. It is not enough to have Latinos in the front lines and in editing positions. We need them in the boardrooms as CEOs. Second, I believe that minority owners tend to be both more sensitive and susceptible to the plight of the community. They speak the same language -- of experience and semantics.

They also tend to have a larger stake in the well being and proper representation of that community.

In later chapters, I also talk about Spanish-language media as advocates for their people. One can argue that all media, in one way or another, serve as advocates for their readers, viewers, and listeners. This role comes naturally and as part of journalism's daily function to highlight worthy events and pinpoint corruption. Hispanic media, as any ethnic media, must play this role even more intensely because they serve a minority. It is, however, not a new role. The first newspapers for Latinos -- as well as blacks, Native Americans, and Asian-Americans -- began in the 19th century in response to crises. They were founded, too, as alternatives to the mainstream press then available. The same holds true today.(1)

I agree with the interviewees who repeatedly said they viewed the media as the voice of their people because in mainstream newspapers and broadcast stations their triumphs and tragedies served only as footnotes. Yet, media can be advocates for their people without breaking with traditional journalistic ethics.

Media can advocate (and that is the purpose of editorial pages), but they cannot allow their reporters to have conflicts of interest (real or perceived). They cannot allow their staff members to receive payments for stories or to moonlight for organizations they cover. They cannot fail to print or air news because it would be harmful to the publisher's friend or to the station's advertising client. They cannot publish or air press releases verbatim, as if the releases were prepared by the outlet's editorial staff.

In a word, advocacy does not rule out the basic tenets of journalism: accuracy, honesty, and thoroughness.

                                                Ana Veciana-Suarez
                                                West Palm Beach, Florida
                                                October 1989

I. Hispanic Media Overview

Spanish-language media are like a kaleidoscope, ever-changing, colorful, and fascinating. To freeze them in time and within pages is nearly impossible, for no sooner has one published a number than it is outdated. No sooner has one predicted a format than it, too, has changed. One thing, however, can be said with some certainty: Hispanic media are growing stronger and attracting more attention, particularly from Corporate America. Where once some predicted their eventual withering, now growth has become the status quo.

Most Hispanic media are located in top urban areas where Hispanics tend to concentrate, though as populations brim over into the suburbs and smaller towns, so too do the media. In small cities once considered too small to support an Hispanic outlet, a radio station and a struggling weekly can often be found.

Much of the action in recent years has been on the national forefront as the two Hispanic networks — Univision and Telemundo — battle for viewers. In radio, Texas State Network's Spanish Information Service has expanded into other states and affiliates in all the major Hispanic markets outside Texas. Lotus' "Radio Noticias/USA TODAY," a five-minute newscast done in partnership with Gannett Co., Inc., was carried by at least 30 stations at the time of this writing. These two radio news services, together with United Press International and Cadena Radio Centro, serve that growing market.

National action in print has been limited to magazines, with the introduction of glossy products that target the upscale, bilingual, better educated Hispanic. Noticias del Mundo, owned by News World Communications Inc., a Unification Church International subsidiary, has seen its hopes of being the first Spanish-language national newspaper dashed. It has not managed to expand to key Hispanic markets such as Miami and other cities in Texas. The emergence of a national newspaper, however, may come from an unlikely source. Macfadden Holdings Inc., the new owner of the National Enquirer, announced in 1989 that it would publish a tabloid a la the Enquirer that would be more specifically of interest to the Spanish-speaking community.

The number of major Spanish-language dailies has remained steady and likely will not change. New York has two -- El Diario/La Prensa and Noticias del Mundo. Los Angeles has two -- La Opinion and Noticias del Mundo. Its third daily, El Diario de Los Angeles, shut down in October 1989. Miami has two -- Diario Las Americas and El Nuevo Herald. Unfortunately, there are no major, widely distributed dailies in Chicago or Texas, two markets that could certainly use them. There are, however, numerous weeklies and monthlies in each of these cities. Some publish sporadically; others have survived for years. A few are trying something new. La Prensa, for example, began weekly publication in July 1989 in San Antonio, a city that badly needed an Hispanic print voice. Most weeklies' circulation figures are unaudited, but it is safe to say that most publish only hundreds or thousands of copies.

Although print is slow to change, there has been a gradual reworking of some formats. La Opinion, for instance, has been slowly adding sections, space, and staff. It has formed an unusual alliance with the Los Angeles Times, and on special occasions has used Times articles, or the Times has published special sections in Spanish. La Opinion helped the Times produce a Spanish-language section on the new U.S. immigration law, for instance. The Times printed about 900,000 extra copies, which were distributed through La Opinion and community groups.

In 1987, Knight-Ridder's Miami Herald launched an improved and enlarged Spanish-language newspaper. Its name was changed slightly from El Herald to El Nuevo Herald, and its newsroom moved from corporate headquarters to a Miami street where other Spanish-language media have their offices.

In the radio market, there are about 220 Spanish-language stations, though that number would be higher if one included brokered stations -- stations with paid programming formats. More radio stations have meant a greater variety of musical formats as well as more segmentation. Even markets not considered traditionally Hispanic -- Atlanta, for instance -- are supporting a Spanish-language radio station. FM is the new name of the game, with the entry of Hispanic FMs in markets such as New York, San Antonio, and Miami making quite a splash. At the time of this writing, New York was expected to get a second Spanish-language FM to compete with Spanish Broadcasting System's WSKQ. Also on the horizon is the increasing practice of simulcasting local news reports of an English-language television station, which will mean more competition for Univision and Telemundo affiliates. The work of WIND-AM in Chicago, in association with WMAQ-TV, is one example of this practice.

Television continued to be a growth market, as Univision and Telemundo sought to increase ad revenues, affiliates, and cable-system carriage. Univision officials claim their network reaches 85 percent of the Hispanic population. Telemundo, the new kid on the block, is not far behind. When it adds its San Antonio station as expected, coverage will be up to 75 percent.

Since 1986, Univision has added affiliates in Reno, Dallas, Albuquerque, Harlingen/Brownsville/McAllen, Tijuana/San Diego, and Yuma/El Centro. These additions bring the number of Univision TV stations to 19. The number of cable systems carrying the network was also up -- to 489, with 55 of those being added between 1988 and 1989.

Telemundo is still playing catch up. It owns and operates television stations in five of the top seven Hispanic markets: Los Angeles, New York, Miami, San Francisco/San Jose, and Houston/Galveston. In addition, its programming is carried in 26 other markets, including Chicago, El Paso, Dallas, Fresno, Albuquerque, and Denver.

With the support of advertisers and audience, both networks have started to produce more domestic programs, many of them quite good -- and quite expensive to produce. Telemundo airs shows such as "Dia a Dia," "Cara a Cara," and "MTV Internacional." It also aired "Angelica, Mi Vida," the first U.S.-produced novela on Hispanics in the United States. Unfortunately, Telemundo falls short in the news department when compared to Univision. Though Telemundo defends its "Noticiero Telemundo-CNN," some view it as a translation of Cable News Network.

Executive producer Marlene May said criticism of the Telemundo-CNN partnership has eased as the product has become better known. "That was criticism you heard at the beginning. Our staff is entirely Hispanic and we're reporting from a Hispanic point of view," she said.

Telemundo has four correspondents in the United States; Univision has twice as many. Telemundo has no permanent reporters outside the country; Univision has four in Latin America. In the past, Telemundo correspondents had to tag along with English-language CNN people or wait for camera and editing time. The numbers showed the shortcomings: Estimates by Strategy Research Corporation in the May 1989 sweeps showed Univision beating Telemundo three to one.

Protests by affiliates, though, have brought about change.(1) CNN is providing more crews and equipment, enabling Telemundo reporters to work with their own editors, producers, and cameras. A network of stringers is being developed in Latin America and elsewhere. International rights to the newscasts had been sold to affiliates in every Central American country, the Dominican Republic, and six South American countries at the time of this writing. More Latin American nations were expected to join.

"When we started," explained May, "the idea was to start small and grow. We have been growing. We've added stringers in Buenos Aires, Costa Rica, Guatemala, and Jerusalem. Eventually we will have stringers in all Latin American countries. We now have state-of-the-art equipment and our reporters are fully independent."

Univision also has its own domestically produced programs: "Cristina," "TV Mujer," and "Portada." With three times the budget, its "Noticiero Univision" is about twice the size of its competitor -- 65 staff members including 14 permanent correspondents. Ten of those are in the United States, the others in Latin America.

Also of interest is ECO, the Spanish-language news and information service which premiered in 1988. ECO airs on Galavision, the cable network that used to show movies, sports, and novelas. It has 300 U.S. affiliates and originates from Mexico City, using journalists from Televisa, that country's largest media business. The news service became the final step in Galavision's transformation from a pay service to a basic channel. With its reach, ECO could become a major media player. However, it is hampered by the fact that it is too regional and does not cover U.S. issues well. It is also competing with rivals Univision and Telemundo. However, if management ever decides to pursue the national U.S. Hispanic market, it could be a force to reckon with.

All of these media may face serious competition from English-language counterparts aiming to attract Hispanics with special programs and bilingual formats. This is true for print as well as radio and television. To wit: the Los Angeles Times began publishing a four-color, broadsheet editorial section in early 1989. The monthly bilingual publication, Nuestro Tiempo, has a circulation of 420,000.

In Miami, NBC affiliate WTJV-TV conducted a $250,000 Spanish radio and press campaign to attract viewers. The other English-language stations have hired more Hispanics and increased their coverage of Hispanic affairs, too. Their actions came on the heels of a special Nielsen report showing that 68 percent of Miami's Hispanics in the 18-to-49 age group watched English-language TV, an increase of 5 percent over two years.

The market is also seeing Hispanic investment in English-language productions. In early 1989, five prominent Hispanics announced the formation of Maravilla Communications, a company that seeks to acquire English-language network-affiliated television stations around the country. Maravilla partners include TV journalist Geraldo Rivera, performer Richard "Cheech" Marin, former New York congressman Herman Badillo, National Hispanic Leadership Conference chairman Tony Bonilla, and Marcelino Miyares, president of Times Square Studios, an independent production facility.

If this group meets with success, it may eventually negate the much-repeated excuse that Hispanics do not have the economic power to own Spanish-language media outlets. If they can team up to buy English stations, they certainly can team up to purchase Spanish ones.

Finally, one of the biggest obstacles Hispanic media must overcome is that of measurements. A Katz Hispanic Radio Research report in the Summer of 1989 underscored the wide variations between Arbitron and Birch, two radio-audience measurement services. Comparing Winter 1989 data in 13 markets, Katz found that Arbitron topped Birch by a range of 6 percent in San Francisco and 111 percent in New York. Birch was higher only in San Diego, by 60 percent.(2) In a Fall 1987 survey of New York stations, Katz also showed wide variations between Strategy Research, Arbitron, and Birch. For example, Strategy Research's Spanish-station CUME (the estimated number of persons who listen to a station for a minimum of five minutes in a quarter hour within a given daypart) was 493 percent higher than Arbitron and 655 percent higher than Birch. Figures for average quarter-hour listening for Spanish stations calculated by Strategy Research were 937 percent higher than Arbitron and 2,357 percent higher than Birch.(3)

There is no consensus on which of the measurements is best. However, Birch, which uses a telephone-recall technique, received the nod from the defunct Spanish Radio Advisory Council.

Other media plagued by such troubling discrepancies have moved to make changes. The National Association of Hispanic Publications (NAHP) has created a "group buy" program in which an advertiser can purchase advertising in several NAHP-member newspapers in a state or region. To participate, the publication's circulation must be verified. Zeke Montes, past president of the organization and a publisher himself, hopes that such an arrangement will entice media owners into independently verifying their circulations. In mid-1989, 95 percent of Hispanic publications did not have audited circulation figures, Montes said.

Also in 1989 Telemundo and Univision joined forces with A.C. Nielsen Co. to track Hispanic TV ratings. At the time of this writing, the boards of the networks had approved a tentative agreement to set up a Hispanic ratings service. The system would be test-marketed in Los Angeles, where plans call for wiring 200 Hispanic homes with "people meters." Once the test was completed, Nielsen would evaluate the system and then institute it across the country in 800 Hispanic homes. The commendable three-way agreement could mean more advertising revenue and, eventually, better programming as that money is invested in domestically produced shows.

"We hope to have half of our programming produced in the United States by 1990 or 1991," said Telemundo President Henry Silverman. "It's a matter of money. When we start getting numbers that are credible, we will have higher revenues and more domestic production. As good as a Venezuelan novela is, how good and topical is it for U.S. Hispanics?"

The media's financial success and, therefore, their very survival may depend on finding ways to produce numbers that can be verified.

Says Meg Bernot, media director of Publiciadad Siboney: "We have to quantify and qualify and stratify everything, even more so than the general markets. We're much more suspect than the others."

II. The Hispanic Market

The Latino population in the United States is an increasingly defined and definable market. Since the 1970s, when the U.S. Bureau of the Census facilitated measurement by including "Hispanic" as a separate category of identification, growth has been staggering. To keep abreast, researchers have measured and surveyed, quantified and qualified -- and come up with some interesting, if not always accurate, numbers.

Possibly one of the most cited reports is the Census Bureau's Hispanic Population in the United States: March 1988 -- an update of the number of Hispanics in this country.(1) From 1980 to 1988, the Hispanic population increased 34 percent (or about five million persons) to a total of 19.4 million. This means Hispanics comprised 8.1 percent of the population, up from 6.5 percent in 1980. The 34-percent increase is even more spectacular when compared to the 6.6-percent growth of non-Hispanics and blacks. The Census Bureau attributes the increase to two factors of roughly equal importance: migration from other countries, and births in the United States.

Population growth rate is particularly important in the discussion of the future of Hispanic media. Eventually, increasing numbers of Hispanics will likely wield considerable political power at the national level, rather than in local government only. This could translate into a proportionate increase in media influence as print and broadcast outlets, already reaching greater numbers of Hispanics, expand their roles as conduits between power brokers and constituents. Furthermore, the steady flow of immigration -- whether legal or illegal -- guarantees a ready, devoted, and dependent audience for Spanish-language media. Even under the most conservative estimates, if half the growth of the Hispanic community is due to immigration, Spanish will remain the language of choice for many, despite the tendency of the children and grandchildren of other Latino immigrants to learn English and assimilate.

The majority of U.S. Hispanics -- 12.1 million or 62 percent -- are of Mexican origin; 2.5 million are of Puerto Rican origin (12.7 percent); 1.035 million are of Cuban origin (5.3 percent); and 3.5 million are of Central and South American origin and from other countries.(2)

Most Hispanics live in five southwestern states. Fifty-five percent live in just two states, California and Texas. These two, along with Arizona, New Mexico, and Colorado, are home to 63 percent of the Hispanic population. Outside the Southwest, New York accounts for 11 percent; Florida for 8 percent; Illinois for 4 percent. What's more, Hispanics tend to congregate geographically by country of origin -- Mexicans in the Southwest, Puerto Ricans in New York, and Cubans in South Florida. Though most live in urban centers, they are following the job markets to the suburbs and to smaller towns.

Hispanic high school and college attainment levels in 1988 were at record levels, according to the census report. Ten percent of Hispanics reported having at least four years of college, compared to 5 percent in 1970. And 51 percent graduated from high school, compared to 32 percent 18 years earlier. These figures are better among younger Hispanics. In the 25-to-34 age group, for example, 62 percent have a high school education compared to 44 percent of their older counterparts.(3) This suggests a better educated Hispanic population, and, in the media's favor, a population that may likely read more newspapers and magazines.

Despite these gains, some serious inequities remain. The national Hispanic dropout rate hovers around 40 percent. Hispanics lag behind non-Hispanics in terms of education, employment levels, and income. The poverty rate of Spanish-origin families in 1987 was almost three times that of non-Hispanic families. More important, it has not changed significantly between 1981 and 1987. Hispanic workers continue to earn less than their counterparts in the labor market and their families continue to have less income than non-Hispanic families.

The 1987 median family income for Latinos, for example, was $20,300 compared to $31,600 for the non-Hispanic population, with Cubans being on the high end of the scale and Puerto Ricans on the low end.(4) Other figures are as disheartening: 26 percent of Hispanic families were below the poverty level in 1987, but only 10 percent of non-Hispanics were. The unemployment rate for Hispanics hovered at the 10-percent level, compared to 7 percent for the rest of the population. And for those with jobs, only 13 percent held managerial or professional positions, compared to 36 percent of non-Hispanics.(5)

Media Use and Language

Media habits often depend on language preference. Those who read, watch, and listen to Spanish-language media tend to be older, more Spanish-dependent, less assimilated and count fewer years of residency in this country. This is especially true of newspaper and television audiences, less so of radio listeners. Focus groups conducted by Menendez International of Miami in early 1989 showed that Los Angeles respondents were the most frequent users of Spanish television -- as measured by average hours of viewing per week. This may be because they are more strongly Spanish dependent. Miami's Hispanics were second, while New York Puerto Ricans reported using Spanish television the least. On the other hand, San Antonians spent an average of 16.1 hours per week listening to Spanish radio, compared to Los Angeles' 14.6, New York's 13.9, and Miami's 11.3.(6)

The use of media is important not only in the fight for ad revenue, but also in the age-old debate of language use. Should media aimed at Hispanics be in Spanish or in English? Not surprisingly, publishers of English-language Hispanic-oriented media argue that the use of English is taking hold at a faster pace than expected, particularly among the more affluent. Thus, the emergence of such publications as Vista and Hispanic magazines. Others, however, insist that Spanish is here to stay. Continued immigration from the south (which accounts for half of Hispanic population growth) and a clinging to culture translates into a steady, if not growing, audience for Spanish-language media. Some research shows that Hispanics rely mainly on the Spanish language, with 90 percent of Hispanics speaking Spanish and only 10 percent speaking English only or primarily.(7) A study published by the Hispanic Policy Development Project in 1988, The Future of the Spanish Language in the United States by Calvin Veltman, concludes that Spanish can survive in the United States only with continued immigration.(8) And since immigration seems to be continuing, it is likely that an audience for Spanish media will remain for some time.

Language becomes particularly important when talking about the young, bilingual Hispanic. Many agree that the 18-to-34 age group prefers English-language media, particularly if they are not new immigrants. When they use Spanish-language media, it is radio first, then television. Research suggests that acculturation and media preference are interdependent. In other words, the more acculturated Hispanics use less Spanish-language media, especially print.(9)

Some, however, do not see this generational gap in media use as a problem. They say U.S. Hispanic media owners could apply some of the different techniques now used in Puerto Rico to the U.S. market, with a few changes.

"You can reach both groups," said George San Jose, of San Jose & Associates in Chicago. "In Puerto Rico, we call one group the 'rockeros' and the other 'salseros.' The rockeros identify more with

Anglo ways, and maybe Anglo media. The salseros identify more with Hispanic culture."

Political Power

Hispanics are an increasingly important political force in the states and urban areas in which they live. Part of their power is reflected in the number of elected officials in office. The National Association of Latino Elected and Appointed Officials (NALEO) in Washington, D.C., has been compiling a roster of Hispanic politicians for six years. This directory has shown a steady increase of 3 to 4 percent each year, according to Luis Baquedano, a research assistant for NALEO. The 1989 roster, to be published in November 1989, shows: 1 governor, 10 members of Congress, 246 mayors, mayors pro tem, or vice mayors. The rest are serving in municipal posts. The toal number of elected Latino officials is 3,783. In 1984, it was 3,128. Because most of these officials are at the entry level of political life -- school board and municipal posts -- Baquedano feels there is "a tremendous pool of future leaders out there."

Growing Hispanic political clout is also expressed in the number of Latinos who are voting. In November 1976, for example, Latinos made up 2.4 percent of the total vote. In 1984, it was 3 percent.(10) By 1988, the Latino vote had increased to 3.6 percent of the total vote, according to the Census Bureau.

Latinos also have the potential to be a determining factor in local congressional races, as the election of Congresswoman Ileana Ros-Lehtinen from Miami in 1989 demonstrates. On a national level, NALEO has concluded that "the Latino population still can have a potentially decisive role" due to Hispanic population concentration.(11) Almost 90 percent of Hispanics live in just nine states, so small shifts in their vote can alter statewide elections as well as influence 193 electoral-college votes. (The nine states in which they live represent 71 percent of the 269 electors needed to win the presidency.) NALEO gives these hypothetical examples:

* "...a shift of just 10.9 percent of the Hispanic voters in Texas from the Democratic candidate to the Republican candidate (with all other factors remaining the same) would reverse the national election with the Republicans winning the presidency."(12)

* "...a change of 10.2 percent of California Hispanic voters and 3.6 percent among New Mexico Hispanic voters from the Republican to Democratic party (again with all else staying the same) would have made the close election into a Democratic landslide in the electoral college."(13)

However, demographic factors -- U.S. citizenship, the relative youth of the Hispanic population, poverty, and low educational attainment -- hamper the political effectiveness of Latinos. One in three U.S.

Hispanics cannot vote because he or she is not a citizen. The growth in this segment of the Latino population has been faster than the growth of the adult U.S. Hispanic citizen population.(14)

Furthermore, because young adults do not participate in elections as frequently as other citizens, the relative youth of the Hispanic population lowers voter participation. The average age of Hispanics is 25 -- compared to 32 for the population as a whole. NALEO sees these two factors as short-term problems. "Active promotion of U.S. citizenship will increase the size of the eligible Latino electorate. While the Latino population will remain younger than average for many years to come, the surge of Hispanics now entering voting age will be passing into the age groups where voting rates are higher."(15)

Poverty and education, though, are two constant factors affecting voting trends. Lower educational attainment and poverty reduce participation in the electoral process, regardless of ethnicity. This has a significant impact on voting patterns of Latinos, who have less education and income than the non-Hispanic population.

Economic Power

Hispanic consumers represent about $130 billion in purchasing power. Large close-knit families, traditional values, brand loyalty, and frequent use of household and food products have attracted advertisers to their media.

Independent research shows that Hispanics tend to place product quality and reputation ahead of price. In Strategy Research Corp.'s 1989 U.S. Hispanic Market study, almost two-thirds agreed that nationally advertised and popular name brands are best for their family. Hispanics used more baby food, breakfast cereal, dessert gelatin/pudding, flour, ice cream, olive oil, rice, bottled water, carbonated soft drinks, coffee, and beer than non-Hispanics. This type of research is vital for Spanish-language media hoping to attract new advertisers.(16)

Advertising Dollars

In an attempt to reach Hispanics, advertisers spent $550.1 million in 1988, the most recent figures available at this writing from Hispanic Business magazine. An overwhelming percentage (almost 46 percent) went to television, which is also true in mainstream media. Nonetheless, radio ad revenue in the Hispanic market is strong because of Hispanic allegiance to that broadcast form. More encouraging than the overall advertising figures are the changes in attitude Hispanic advertising agencies have noticed among their clients.

"Hispanic media is no longer a token buy," said Marcelino Miyares Jr., media director of the Unimar agency in Chicago. "There is a trend to become more Americanized, more like the general market."

Meg Bernot, media director of Publicidad Siboney in New York, agrees with Miyares. She reports that clients "are more serious about this market. They are more demanding." Siboney's clients, including Colgate-Palmolive and Pepsi, expect results -- product sales -- not simply pats on the back or recognition from Latino leaders.

Nonetheless, advertising to Hispanics is not nearly what it could be. Though Hispanics make up 8 percent of the population, spending on Hispanic media by advertisers does not even come close. Industry figures put it at about 1 percent of total ad dollars, though some companies, especially those that sell household products, toiletries, and foods, may spend more. Some agency executives have resigned themselves to the likelihood that the percentage of advertising dollars earmarked for Hispanic media in the United States will never match the percentage of Hispanics in the general population. The oversimplification of this model notwithstanding, it would not be fair to expect such a "matching" ratio because some Hispanics can also be reached through the general media. Predictably, however, both media owners and agency media directors agree that billings should increase. Certainly, steady income can translate into better quality and more independence -- two things that Spanish-language media need badly.

III. The National Agenda

The question of media power is as old as the first orator, as timeless as the printed word. In different fields and in different contexts, media critics, owners, and consumers wonder: Does TV violence make for more violent children? Do editorials and other political endorsements influence our voting patterns? Does quoting a person repeatedly make him a leader and expert in the public's eye? How much influence does a newspaper, a radio station, a television show really have on our buying, eating, loving, working, and dressing habits? And can it be measured?

The mass media are essential to a free and democratic society. In America, they have played a vital role in history. As researcher David Ramsey put it, "In establishing American independence, the pen and the press had a merit equal to that of the sword."(1) Certainly such importance can be placed on some media today, whether in English or in Spanish. What's more, Spanish-language media must play an additional role, as must all minority media, or media that serve an underclass. Ethnic media must provide information and entertainment, of course, but that is just one facet of their business. They must also serve as champion, crusader, advocate. They are the voice of an audience that may have neither voting power nor economic strength. They are the ones who must point out injustices, expose prejudices, open recalcitrant doors, salute triumphs. This is true of mainstream media to a certain extent, but it is especially important for minority newspapers and broadcast outlets. Their readers and listeners often have no other recourse.

"They should serve differently because we're not being served by the mainstream media," said Marta Ayala, who was director of program services for the Mayor's Advisory Commission on Latino Affairs in Chicago in early 1989. "Nobody is recording our history unless our media do it."

The Spanish-language media in the top Hispanic markets the author visited -- Los Angeles, New York, Miami, San Antonio, and Chicago -- fill their role of crusader in a sometimes schizophrenic manner. Some do it better than others, by excellent editorials, informative inserts, top-notch reporting, and accurate portrayal of the many wrongs in their communities. Most, however, do it sporadically and on a very simple level. In other words, they air the public-service announcements and publish the press releases but do not go beyond the surface. They cover a conference on gang violence, but do not cover on a consistent basis the societal problems that lead to gangs. This requires resources that some do not have or are not willing to invest.

However, the perception by leaders of the role Hispanic media should play in their communities -- as well as on a national level -- raises an ethical question that is at the heart of ongoing journalistic debate: Should newspapers, radio, and television stations be detached observers of our daily lives? Or should they be leaders, molders of opinion? Hispanic audiences want both. They want newspapers that expose corruption as well as publish "good stories" about Latinos who have made it within the current power structure. They want media to reinforce customs and promote Hispanic values while also exposing the audience to the American way of life by raising aspirations and instructing them about surviving in an increasingly bureaucratic system. In a sense, leaders interviewed for this book wanted the media to be judge and jury, prosecutor and defense attorney.

"Spanish-language media," proposed Estella Romero, a Los Angeles-area businesswoman who runs Estella Romero Enterprises, a marketing firm, "have a more extensive role by the very nature of the people they serve. They must be more involved in disseminating information, in educating, and in advocacy. That may not fit in with what some people see as the traditional role of media in this country, but Spanish media are not traditional in that sense."

In interviews in five major Hispanic markets with business people, community leaders, appointed officials, elected politicians, and media executives, it was not always easy to establish a cause-and-effect relationship between an outlet's stories (or editorial campaigns) and a resulting change -- in policy, attitude, or structure. It is even more difficult to make blanket statements about Hispanic media's influence and impact on a national level. Generally, effects vary according to issue, region, and medium used.

A medium's acceptance within a community depends on several factors -- namely, its credibility and reach, its style of presentation, and the message itself. The first two are in an adolescent stage for most Hispanic media, though improved reporting, responsible editorializing, and better forms of measurement are making strides in the right direction. As for the message, politicians and grassroots leaders alike agree that Hispanic media -- like many of their Anglo counterparts -- rarely take stands on controversial subjects. The media tend to be followers, not leaders.

What Spanish-language media do well, almost in spite of themselves, is to serve as liaison and window between the different groups that make up Hispanic U.S.A. Primarily because of network television, the Mexican-Americans in the Southwest know more about the Cuban-Americans in the Southeast who, in turn, know more about the Puerto Ricans in the Northeast. Like its English-language counterpart of 30 years ago, Spanish-language TV (and radio and newspapers to a lesser extent) has helped expand the horizons of the audience, providing views they normally would not have seen. It has also -- for better or for worse, depending on whom you ask -- somewhat homogenized this very diverse and extensive population known as U.S. Hispanics.

There is no question that media individually and collectively are influential. How much, with whom, and how often, are debatable -- and unprovable -- questions. Nonetheless, mass media have traditionally played a very important role in changing America, and Spanish-language newspapers, radio, and television stations are no exception. They influence what we think about, the way we dress, what we buy, and, in certain instances, how we vote. They make heroes -- or anti-heroes, as the case may be -- of unknown figures almost overnight. They transform local happenings into world events. And, just as important, they have subtly, subliminally determined the socialization and habits of an entire generation.

Generally, the power of Spanish-language media in any one location depends on three factors: Hispanics' economic power in that particular city, area, or region; their political power; and the retention of the language. One factor alone is not enough to give media power. For instance, in San Antonio, a city where the political clout of Hispanics is strong and the economic power growing, the retention of Spanish is not as high as in other areas. (Many San Antonians are third- and fourth-generation Mexican-Americans.) The Spanish-language media there are far from strong. In Miami, on the other hand, where all three factors are at work, Spanish-language newspapers and broadcast stations play an important and influential role not only in the Latin community but in mainstream circles as well. The same holds true in varying degrees in Los Angeles and New York.

Yet, one cannot draw ironclad conclusions about media effects because too often their influence wanes or grows with the issue and the availability of the medium itself. A newspaper, for instance, may be more influential in getting a borough president to set up a task force to study living conditions in a neighborhood -- as was the case in New York -- but television sells a product and an "instantaneous idea" more easily to the public.(2) Researcher Bernard Berelson expressed this occasional influence in 1949 when he came up with the following axiom:

"Some kinds of communication on some kinds of issues, brought to the attention of some kinds of people under some kinds of conditions, have some kinds of effects."(3)

Tom Sharpe, director of public information for the National Council of La Raza, has had mixed results with the Spanish-language media, leading him to conclude that there is a selective perception and reception by the audience. In other words, even when media coverage of different issues is equal, audience response is not.

"The issue itself is what gets the most response," Sharpe said. "That seems to me the strongest variable."

Sharpe cited a 1988 press conference the Council held on the volatile issue of Hispanics and housing. For months afterward, people were still calling for information and congressmen were quoting from the report. "I don't know if there was a statute change anywhere, but it certainly increased public awareness," he added.

Spanish-language media exercise their influence most strongly among the Spanish-dependent recent arrivals who have no other source of information and rely solely on the local diario or radio. Researchers at the University of Texas at Austin in 1985 concluded in a survey of Texas Hispanics that socioeconomic status and cultural identification can predict Spanish-language media use. Basically, those using these media most are persons with a low education, who belong to the low income bracket, who are elderly, and who have a high cultural identification."(4) They are a faithful audience, more so than the more assimilated Latinos. To wit: an Univision special on Nicaragua garnered a 50-percent higher rating in Miami, which is predominantly Cuban, than a special on Cuba, though they aired at the same time and day two weeks apart.

Spanish-language media, by the same token, have less impact on the bilingual, more assimilated Hispanic who gets information from a variety of sources. He or she is often the Latino in a position of political, economic, or social power. But the media's limited audience within this group may not always be the fault of their coverage or the concerted efforts of managers. The lack of time was often cited as a factor when those interviewed said they did not use Latino media as often.

"If I'm pressed for time, I pick up the Los Angeles Times," said Estella Romero, the businesswoman who runs her own marketing firm. "If you're successful or want to be successful, you want to be reading what everybody else is reading. You want to be quoting from the Times, not La Opinion. If they read La Opinion, they also are reading the Times."

Spanish media also have less, if any, influence within the context of general society. Because only a subset of this society is able to use these media, they cannot have the power of their mainstream counterparts with similar content and form.

Lionel Sosa, of Sosa & Associates ad agency in San Antonio, suggests that media must pass through three stages of development before having a truly measurable impact on the audience. In the first stage, a medium must keep itself alive. Its main purpose is to survive, to bring in ad revenues, to have a positive cash flow. Gradually, as this occurs, it will also inform the public (stage two). The third stage is the development of influence. Many media outlets, though, reach this final point in a haphazard way and not because of a concerted effort. As Sosa remarked, "It's more 'I will if I can.'"

Though most Spanish media are only in their second stage of development, they probably have influenced their audiences on a local and even national level. But that influence has generally been of the most basic kind -- prompting the audience to imitate a fashion, to admire a new celebrity. In short, they can play a role in purchasing decisions. Influence of the more complicated kind -- community mobilization, government policy change, heeding of a message by public officials -- is much more difficult to document. This social, political, and cultural influence can be felt strongly within the Hispanic community but less intensely outside that community.

One Sosa & Associates Spanish media campaign, for instance, increased the penetration of a cable company from 39 percent to 57 percent of Hispanic households in one year. It is much more difficult to measure impact of a news story on the community. Only on occasion is there a clear cause-and-effect relationship--for example, when a radio station deejay pleads for donations for victims of the Puerto Rican mudslides, and the community responds with fervor and plenty of money and canned goods.

Broadcast media are pervasive and consequently vital to advertisers in introducing and selling a product. However, this does not necessarily hold true for the promotion of a political movement or idea. Where advertising executives repeatedly cited television as the most influential medium, Hispanic community leaders and politicians, by and large, said they were more influenced by Spanish-language print because of its sustained coverage of local community projects and the space and effort it devotes to news.

In the cities where newspapers exist, the printed word seems to carry the most impact. In Los Angeles, community leaders cited La Opinion in most, if not all, of their examples of media influence. The same was true in New York, with El Diario/La Prensa. In Miami, a revamped El Nuevo Herald had a strong influence, though at times it was overshadowed by television and the Spanish-language news-formatted radio stations in that city. But in the cities where there are no widely distributed, credible newspapers -- Chicago and San Antonio -- Spanish media as a whole did not emerge as an influential force, according to the leaders and opinions molders interviewed. Radio and television -- perhaps because they are so entertainment driven, perhaps because they fragment their audience -- did not make up for the lack of news/public affairs programming in these cities.

The power of newspapers in Miami, Los Angeles, and New York came as no surprise. Even though the print media do not reach nearly as many people as the electronic outlets, they tend to appeal more to an elite. Leaders were more likely to read a good Spanish-language daily such as La Opinion than to watch Spanish-language television. More important, a newspaper can sustain continual coverage of an issue. It editorializes and devotes much of its resources to the business of news. One of its stories or columns can be easily copied, passed around, and quoted. Furthermore, while New York, Los Angeles, and Miami had at least two Spanish-language dailies, only one in each city was clearly the most influential and effective.

Non-traditional print media, such as the Hispanic Link Weekly Report, provide an excellent example of influence to a select group -- a small but powerful cadre of politicians, grassroots leaders, writers, journalists, and businessmen. Sharpe of La Raza said if he were limited to one medium, he would likely use Hispanic Link.

"Hispanic Link has an incredible ripple effect," he said. "It's the best concise, boiled-down newsletter of its type. A lot of people in the media and people who wield power pick it up. What it sometimes comes down to is not the large numbers but the type of people you do reach."

On the other hand, there is no medium like broadcast for quick exposure, for widening horizons, for easy use. In the case of a city like Miami, where about half the Spanish radio stations have news formats, and television stations have pioneered and devoted their resources to news and public-affairs programming, broadcast stations can mobilize a community very quickly.

Explained Carlos Arboleya, Barnett Banks' vice chairman and Miami community leader: "The power of the (radio) stations in Miami is such that they can initiate any community endeavor, including unrest, within six hours."

In some cities, the older, established radio stations exercise considerable influence, particularly through individual air personalities who are admired by the community. These commentators are looked upon for guidance. In San Antonio, the late Mateo Camargo who hosted "La Hora de la Sopa" on KCOR was considered such a leader, his suggestions taken seriously, his recommendations followed.

On a national level, few, if any media, have an impact on government policy. (The exceptions are the networks.) But on a local level they have prompted people to register to vote, to apply for political asylum, to stand up and be counted in the census. They can mobilize some of their audiences on some of the issues, but they do not necessarily mobilize the non-Hispanic national leaders.

That is changing, though, as Hispanics' political clout grows. Congressman Esteban Torres (D-Calif.) recounts that more and more non-Hispanic congressmen tell him they are learning Spanish.

"The media are not there yet, but there are increasing signs that we are getting there," Torres said. "Like everything else Hispanic, they're reaching a crescendo level."

If a Spanish-language medium is to emerge on a national level, it likely will be Univision or Telemundo. More and more politicians in Washington are watching Spanish-language television as more of their constituents turn out to be Latinos, Torres said. Already network television has shown bright and hopeful signs of muscle flexing. TV was instrumental in informing viewers about the amnesty provisions of the immigration law. It helped convince Hispanics it was all right to apply for amnesty. "It has had a tremendous impact on that issue," Torres said. "I see the networks as being very effective."

A gambler would bet on Univision because of its track record, management, and commitment to programming. As long as rival Telemundo continues to farm out its news programming, it cannot expect to win a sincere following. Too many Latinos consider the Spanish-language CNN/Noticiero product on Telemundo a translation of English-language CNN, lacking in cultural authenticity.

However, Univision is not nearly as influential now as it could be. An over-dependence on telenovelas and foreign programming has turned away the young, bilingual Hispanics, many of whom exercise considerable political and economic power in the mainstream arena. Leaders interviewed for this book complained about the lack of a regular Nightline/Ted Koppel program that would go beyond the news. In most cases, they did not consider the networks a force on the national level, and mentioned them only when prompted.

Ilya Adler, a professor at the University of Illinois in Chicago and a former editor, claims it is highly probable that Univision and Telemundo will, in time, be very influential. In a few years, the Spanish-language networks of the latter '80s will be compared to the English-language networks of the '50s.

"We will talk about them like we do about CBS, ABC, and NBC, but that will happen down the line, not now," he said. "It's too soon. They're both too young and with new owners."

Guillermo Martinez, Univision executive news director, admits that Univision has not yet managed to gain national influence through appropriate programming. "The only power we have now is at the local level," he said. "We know that. But it is difficult to influence three different groups -- Cubans, Mexicans, and Puerto Ricans -- in the same way."

He promises the network will continue to move away from imported programming and produce more news magazine shows. In the first six months of 1989, Univision had aired 10 documentary-type news magazine shows.

Telemundo President Henry Silverman's goal is to have one-half of the network's programming domestically produced by 1991. The advent of better audience measurement will bring more ad revenues that will, in turn, be invested in better programming, he added.

All Spanish-language media, whether network television or local newspaper, wield power in a variety of ways:

* **By influencing policy makers and opinion molders.** Newspapers and broadcast outlets often expose power brokers to another point of view or offer solutions -- and sometimes even scare them into changing or acting.

* **Serving as a means of communication between those who have political and economic power and the public they serve.** Just as an elected official uses the media to get the message across to constituents -- be it a pet project or simply a plea for votes at election time -- the media can serve as a conduit for the message of the people to the halls of power.

* **Mobilizing the community.** Media outlets can persuade their audiences to call their councilmen, write their congressmen, complain to government agencies, boycott businesses. Eliciting reaction of any kind, be it good or bad, frivolous or serious, is a barometer of power.

* **Changing attitudes and values within the community.** In some cases, particularly in those of immigrants newly exposed to issues and circumstances, media help to form opinions on new experiences.

* **Creating leaders and legitimizing unknown grassroots movements.** All media regularly confer leadership status simply by the repeated use of certain "spokesmen," the play of stories, and continual treatment of a particular subject through followups, editorials, and feature and news stories.

Influencing policy makers and opinion molders is probably the most difficult and unmeasurable of these indices. In the case of Spanish media, their range is limited because of language. Unless the person in power speaks or reads Spanish, it is likely that he or she is not exposed to the medium. That, however, is quickly changing, and not only on a national level as explained previously. Anglo officials in large urban Hispanic areas invariably have Latino aides and/or Hispanic commissions and offices. New York and Chicago both do, for example. In addition, more and more of those in power are Latinos who are familiar with Spanish-language media and use them to gauge interest in issues. Thus, coverage by New York's El Diario/La Prensa motivated Bronx Borough President Fernando Ferrer to appoint a commission to study the problems in one neighborhood.

Perhaps the most obvious exercise of power is the use of media by government and other leaders to communicate a message to Hispanics. It is virtually impossible to run a political campaign in the Hispanic markets without using Spanish-language media. It is as difficult, too, to run any type of campaign, be it a lake cleanup, free vaccination program, or community barbecue, without using them. However, Spanish media alone cannot get the job done. If one wants to reach Latinos with varying degrees of language proficiency and assimilation, one must use the English-language media. This is particularly true if the target audience is young Latinos. One of the Spanish media's biggest problems is their inability to reach the younger, bilingual market.

Like the English-language media, their success in mobilizing the community varies greatly, depending on the issue, the medium, and the city. They do well in bringing out audiences for promotional events -- parties, concerts, even fundraisers. But they do poorly in eliciting response for what community leaders consider "serious" conferences. That, however, may not be an accurate measure of media power as much as a reflection of community apathy.

Readers interviewed disagreed on the extent to which the media help change attitudes. Generally, all media, regardless of language, help to develop attitudes only when the audience has not already formed an opinion. In other words, an endorsement may be considered a useful feather in the hat for a politician, but it probably persuades only a few of the undecided, not those who plan to vote against him. Media, however, serve as reinforcers of customs and culture. They publish special issues on dates of historical interest to various Hispanic groups. They sponsor cultural events. They instill pride in the Latino heritage.

There is, of course, a reciprocal effect in the media-audience equation. Just as newspapers and broadcast stations influence their audiences, so, too, can readers and listeners have an impact on the media. The simplest way is by the act of consuming -- or not consuming -- the product. A reader can opt not to buy a newspaper. He can switch channels, or change radio stations. Because the media (and their advertisers) depend on the numbers, the ultimate power truly lies in the hands of the audience. Yet such power is not always exercised. The lack of alternatives may force an audience to use a medium it does not respect. Too many outlets have waited too long to improve, and then done so only because of the specter of competition on the horizon or the reaction of dissatisfied readers and viewers.

"The power is there, but it is not being used right," complained Anita Villarreal, president of the Little Village Chamber of Commerce in Chicago. "They (the media) react only when forced to. But sooner or later, the community is going to get together and say, 'If you don't do this, we're going to stop advertising. If you don't do this, we're not going to read you or watch you.'"

To give credit where credit is due: Spanish-language media do some things quite well. They are excellent sources of Latin American news, though not always national or local news. They serve as a vehicle of information and a source of pride for a disenfranchised group. They provide a forum for emerging minority leaders and a window into the United States for immigrants. But they must also take the blame for shoddy reporting and unoriginal journalism, a lack of responsibility and an often condescending attitude toward the audience. They do not take risks and are content to leave things as they are. Those that make money do not always reinvest to make a better product. And those that don't, have not achieved the economic independence that would allow them to criticize those who use, patronize, and oppress their people.

Summarizing from interviews for this book and the author's observations, the media's faults include:

* A lack of vision and aggressiveness.

* Few investigative or explanatory pieces.

* Failure to attract a young, bilingual audience.

* Failure to cover local issues in a thorough manner.

* Few domestically produced broadcast programs.

* An inability -- or unwillingness -- to cultivate a skilled, experienced cadre of reporters to provide continuity and perspective in coverage.

There are notable exceptions. La Opinion, the oldest daily Spanish-language newspaper, was constantly cited by Los Angeles leaders and readers for its coverage of local and national issues, its journalistic improvement in recent years, and commitment to the community. In Miami, El Nuevo Herald, which has had a long antagonistic relationship with the Cuban community, garnered some favorable reviews, as did some of that city's news radio stations. Univision's network news, as well as a few of its owned-and-operated stations, were also given nods of approval. Telemundo produced its first U.S. novela, and a few other outlets were slowly but steadily improving. These, unfortunately, tended to be in the minority.

Even outlets which had improved admitted the need for more work. "We need to improve our economic coverage. And we are lacking in European, Asian, and African news because we have no correspondents. I also would like to see us do more vignettes of life in America," Univision's Martinez said.

Finally, the question of ownership and control emerged as a bone of contention in almost every conversation during research for this book. Corporate America, and not Hispanic America, is the owner of traditional Hispanic media. Two of the five daily newspapers, both television networks, and most of the radio stations are owned by public and private U.S. companies. In the Summer of 1989, El Diario/La Prensa of New York was sold by Gannett Co., Inc., to a local partnership that includes the newspaper's publisher, Carlos Ramirez. Of the other larger media, only La Opinion, owned by the Lozano family; Diario Las Americas, owned by the Aguirres; Spanish Broadcasting System, a radio network under Raul Alarcon, Jr.; and Mambisa Corporation, another broadcasting entity headed by Amancio Suarez, are controlled by U.S. Hispanics. The trend toward consolidation means that the power over the flow of information is in the hands of only a few corporations, some of which have neither Hispanics on their boards nor a vested interest in the community they serve. Several leaders likened this situation to the white entertainment industry's exploitation of black entertainers in the early 1960s. Sadly for Hispanics, ownership of Hispanic media by large, Anglo corporations is not likely to change any time soon, considering the amounts being paid for outlets and the leverage needed to run them.

Furthermore, factional fighting among the different ethnic groups threatened to divide the few gains network managements had instituted in programming. During 1989, Mexican-Americans protested the "Cubanization" of the two networks, saying that both Univision and Telemundo favored Cubans in hiring and in programming, although Mexican-Americans are by far the largest audience. The programming, protesters added, lacked relevance for the blue-collar working-class Mexican population. The brunt of the complaints fell on the Los Angeles stations -- KMEX and KVEA -- although the networks themselves did not escape the criticism.(5)

Both Univision and Telemundo have refuted the charges, pointing out that the bulk of their programming is imported from Mexico. However, some of the protesters' criticisms were well founded. Telemundo, owned by Reliance Group Holdings, had no Hispanics on the board of directors until recently. At the time of this writing, it had appointed two -- a Mexican-American and a Cuban-American. It has one Cuban-American in upper management, the senior vice president for programming. Univision, owned by Hallmark, Inc., does a bit better. Eight high-ranking executives are Latino; four of these eight are Cuban-Americans, three are from South America and one is Mexican-American. Not one is Puerto Rican. Five of the nine general managers heading full-power Univision stations are Mexican-Americans. But as at Telemundo, the top two to three posts are held by non-Hispanics.

That this Cubanization has resulted in a deterioration in programming, however, may not be true. Since Telemundo and Univision entered the market, domestically produced programming has increased and the result has been better Spanish-language television, more reflective of U.S. Latinos. That is not to say that this programming does not need to get better. There is much room for improvement to make shows more sensitive to Mexican-American concerns, without discriminating against other Latino groups.

Cuban-American managers have privately expressed concerns about facing prejudice as a minority within a minority. And network television executives say they do not want to engage in reverse discrimination.

"It's reverse racism," Telemundo President Silverman explained. "I'm not asking people where they're from when I hire them. We hire the best people possible. I don't care if they're black, blue, or white, Mexican or Cuban."

Telemundo's programming, he added, is "an attempt to be as broad based as possible." Both networks produce in Miami because costs are lower in Florida, a non-union state.

The infighting among diverse Latino groups unfortunately may shift the focus away from the real concerns in Spanish-language media: growing Anglo ownership and few domestically produced programs. Power still lies in the hands which control the purse strings. Those who believe that editorial independence can overcome any type of ownership, however, would do well to listen to the Bronx-born-and-bred Fernando Ferrer: "The myth of editorial independence is just that -- a myth. Owners do indeed have the control. The power still rests with whoever buys the ink by the barrel."

IV. Los Angeles

The Market

Los Angeles is the top Hispanic market in the United States, with an estimated 4.459 million Latinos, according to Strategy Research Corporation's 1989 market report. This group makes up 19 percent of the total U.S. Hispanic population. As a matter of fact, the Los Angeles-area Latino population alone is so large that it would be the eighth-largest metro area in this country -- bigger than Houston, Atlanta, or Dallas.

The market is young; 37 percent is under 18 years old. Seventy-five percent are of Mexican background. Those from Central America make up 19 percent of the population. The average residency is 11 years, 9 months.(1)

The Media

Los Angeles is home to the oldest Spanish-language newspaper, as well as one of the more successful television stations. La Opinion was founded in September 1926 and is still run today by the Lozano family. A recent move to new headquarters and consistent editorial improvements have made it into a newspaper Los Angeles Hispanic leaders consider their medium of record. The second daily is Noticias del Mundo, which also publishes in other cities. A third, El Diario de los Angeles, which began in May 1987, stopped publication in October 1989. There are also several weeklies.

In early 1989, the Los Angeles Times began publishing a bilingual broadsheet called Nuestro Tiempo. The monthly insert includes coverage of sports, arts, and entertainment, as well as feature stories on community groups and personalities. Every item appears both in English and in Spanish. Nuestro Tiempo is distributed to Times subscribers in areas of Los Angeles and Orange counties with a high Latino population.

In addition to the print media, full-time Spanish-language radio stations serving this market include: KALI, KLVE-FM, KTNQ, KSKQ, and KWKW. In television, KMEX, the Univision station, is the oldest and usually the ratings leader. KVEA, a Telemundo station, signed on in November 1985.

The Power

Spanish-language media in Los Angeles are powerful at a grassroots level, but such power is limited by language and other factors. They influence the way the audience thinks and behaves, they have molded listening and living habits, they have provided a forum for Latino leaders, and, on occasion, affected the policymaking process of government. They draw much of their power from the huge population and from their generally good coverage of certain issues. Yet, the power of Latino media in Los Angeles -- with a couple of exceptions -- tends to be an isolated phenomenon. Like Latino media in other cities, their impact on the broad spectrum of society occurs only when the issues they have long covered are picked up by their English-language counterparts.

Of course, this is true in almost all other top Hispanic markets, especially those in which the large population of Hispanics does not have the economic and political clout that matches its size. For instance, La Opinion -- well respected among Hispanic leaders interviewed -- did extensive reporting on health care for the undocumented. But "public officials don't always read La Opinion," lamented councilwoman Gloria Molina, who does. "Only when (health care) started being covered by the general media did I see their points as part of the process of change." Most officials tend to be Anglos.

Because Los Angeles is a young market with so many recent arrivals, many elected and appointed officials have wrongly ignored the non-voting public. Yet, the Spanish-language media draw most of their audience from that universe. Added Molina, "Are their editorials listened to? No. There is still an arrogance by many of our elected officials that this is an insignificant community when it comes to the reality of voting."

David Lopez Lee, a professor in the School of Public Administration at USC, explains that politicians or aspiring politicians may ignore the Spanish-language media because it does not prove to be time effective to be concerned with them. "The bulk of Spanish-speakers are not registered to vote. On a time-efficient basis, they work with the media that have greater access," he said. "In addition, a lot of elected officials, even if they speak Spanish, may feel more comfortable in English."

Much of the ignorance on the part of public officials is changing, and not all politicians fit so snugly into one caste. Elena Valencia, who worked for Senator David Roberti, president pro tempore of the California State Senate, reported that one of her responsibilities was to look at the Spanish-language newspapers every day. "If I saw an issue that he had to be aware of, it would be teletyped to his office. I think we're seeing more Hispanic staff people who keep track of the media."

The media's lack of influence arises largely because many outlets have targeted their markets too narrowly, almost to the exclusion of bilingual, more assimilated Hispanics. This is not an uncommon complaint. Leaders in every other city voiced the same dissatisfaction with Spanish-language newspapers, radio, and television stations whether they were on the East Coast or the West. To reach the young bilinguals of L.A. -- or any other city, for that matter -- one must send the message through a medium they use.

Valencia has run the Volunteer Center of East/Northeast Los Angeles, a social service agency, since July 1987. She must use the media often to make sure her events are attended, that free or reduced-fee services are used, and that the public is informed about a variety of helpful programs. In 1989, a measles epidemic broke out in Los Angeles County. Sixty percent of the measles cases were Hispanic children. Her staff quickly sent out press releases and public-service announcements informing Latinos that their children had to be immunized.

"We had to do the PSAs in Spanish but also on the 'now-sound' English stations to make sure we were reaching our people," she said. "There is no way you can use one without the other."

Yet, even those who say they do not always read La Opinion or listen to KTNQ or watch KMEX admit that L.A.'s Spanish-language media have improved dramatically, and that, in several cases, they are the ones which cover certain issues more extensively and with greater insight.

"La Opinion is influential when it scoops a story, and it has done so several times," said John Huerta, general counsel for the Hispanic Media Coalition, a volunteer advocacy group that strives to improve the Latino image in media and among employers. "It has a secondary impact on the broadcast media. English media work the same way. If you're not in the Times, you usually won't make it on the 6 p.m. news. Newspapers set the agenda for what's going to be covered."

Arturo Madrid, an educator and president of the Tomas Rivera Center, maintains that media are often influential in spite of themselves and on a level not easily recognizable by those who sit in judgment. They influence how people think and act and not so much how they vote, which is the only barometer of power for most politicians. "The real power of media," adds Rivera, "is to influence people to buy, to act, to behave -- sometimes against their best self-interest."

Estela Scarlata, production manager and co-founder of the Bilingual Foundation of the Arts, maintains the media influence an audience only if that audience wants to be influenced. In other words, readers and viewers have to be predisposed to an idea, open to a new concept on which they have not yet formed an opinion. The idea -- or in the case of advertising, a product -- must be readily accessible and easy to use or understand. The more difficult it is, the fewer chances of having it be accepted or used. Thus, Spanish-language media in Los Angeles can bring out the crowds for a festival, but not for an opera despite the same number of stories, advertisements, or public-service announcements. This is not necessarily a reflection of media power (or lack thereof) but of societal values. The same is true for English media.

"Media power fluctuates," Scarlata said. "They can mobilize a community depending on the issue. If it's a festival or a couple of people playing the maracas and offering a little beer, it will move people. But if it's a cultural thing or the event at the university, you're not going to see the same results."

La Opinion clearly emerged as the outlet with the most influence in Latino L.A. This may be because of its longevity. La Opinion is well known and respected. It has undergone several changes and additions that have made it a better paper. Much of its power may also be derived from the very nature of the print medium which allows for sustained coverage of issues. The newspaper's coverage of health care of undocumented aliens won kudos from leaders for sensitive, responsible journalism. The newspaper also worked with the Los Angeles Times to produce special bilingual issues on the new immigration law in 1988. The inserts were included in La Opinion as well as in the Los Angeles Times. It also put together a supplement on AIDS that was packed with information.

Going that extra mile with special publications has won the admiration of leaders who believe it is likely that La Opinion's audience has been well served. As a matter of fact, many readers may have got their only information on AIDS and immigration law changes through that newspaper. Such work is commendable because it likely brings about change -- in awareness and attitude -- on a grassroots level. However, La Opinion's editorials are not translated into English, which makes its accessibility to English-speakers more of a stumbling block than with other Spanish-language dailies which translate their editorials.

Radio and television are excellent vehicles by which politicians can project an image, advertisers can sell a product, and promoters can generate interest in an event. But exposure to news items is limited by the very content of the media themselves. In other words, broadcast's pervasiveness is offset by its overwhelming entertainment-driven programming. Yes, a novela exposes its audience to a new segment of society, a different setting, or alternative lifestyles. The audience, in turn, may imitate certain habits of dress, mannerisms, and, in certain instances, more serious behavior. However, the limited time

Los Angeles radio and television stations lend to news and public-affairs programming (compared to La Opinion or another daily) dilutes those outlets' ability to be a force for change.

"Radio news is very event oriented except for public-affairs shows," explained Alicia Maldonado, director of communications for the Mexican-American Legal Defense and Educational Fund (MALDEF) in Los Angeles. "TV, unless it's public affairs or election analysis, stays more superficial. You do not get much analysis; maybe it's because they lack time or manpower."

Yet the broadcast media are not without their successes. MALDEF teamed up with Univision (Channel 34 in Los Angeles) for a massive national education program on the 1990 Census. And the local outlets of both Univision and Telemundo did stories on police brutality and street vendors.

"That, in a sense, was a scoop for them," councilwoman Molina said. "They were the first to expose the problems, before other media. In the case of the street vendors, the exposure came when we were trying to formulate a policy to regulate them. After their stories there was more appreciation of who these people were, people who normally would be considered culprits."

The Spanish-language television stories also sparked an interest from the mainstream media, which covered the dilemma of street vendors trying to make a living. Those stories were the ones which brought about this "appreciation" by policy makers that Molina mentions. But again, the power of Spanish-language media is felt on a higher level only with the help of their English-language counterparts.

The Impact

In a city as sizable and populous as Los Angeles, power of any kind tends to be segmented and diluted, be it power of the media, an institution, or a leader. Because of this diffusion, Spanish-language media play an important role within the specific community they serve but a diminished one within the greater society. They perform their principal power roles admirably: as a voice of a people, a forum for their leaders, and a spotlight for varying ideas and interests. What would be a footnote in mainstream media sometimes receives front-page treatment in Spanish-language newspapers or a top-of-the-lineup spot on television. Community activists who would be ignored in English are included in stories in Spanish.

Without the media, many grassroots movements would lose momentum. Some would not succeed. One that succeeded was the fight by residents in East Los Angeles to prevent the government from placing a prison in their neighborhood. Councilwoman Molina believed the media played a vital role in promoting the residents' cause. They legitimized the group, Mothers of East Los Angeles, drew attention to the concerns, and ultimately sided with them.

"They have covered our protests, our issues, our conferences. The coverage by the Spanish-language media was very complete," she said.

Such coverage, added Valencia of the Volunteer Center, highlighted the community's fight in a way that allowed public officials to gauge the volatility of the issue as high. "Media," she said, "give a certain weight to whatever they cover. They make it seem more important."

The Problems

Though Los Angeles' Spanish-language media are among the best in the country, they are not immune to problems that plague outlets elsewhere. Yet one thing can be said for most of them. Managements seem to display an interest in improving, in doing better, in serving the community on a higher level. Though all media are ruled by the bottom line, and it would be Pollyannaish to think money is not important, the general feeling of most leaders interviewed was that the media have a stake in the Latino community and care what happens to it.

Many of the improvements have come about under new owners or managers, because of competition or the realization that change was needed. But come about they have.

"Years ago," recalled Molina, "it was just wire stories and translations of the news. Now there are editors who understand local issues. The reporters are well informed and persistent. They follow the issues. As a matter of fact, Channels 34 and 52 and La Opinion have City Hall reporters."

Radio was perhaps the one medium that received the most criticism, mainly because some of the stations devote little time to news or public-affairs programming, and when they do, it is during low listening hours. Valencia expressed the dismay of others when she blurted during an interview: "Enough! Enough of the dances and the salsa and the music. That's the money part. But I think they need to cover the serious issues. When there's an outbreak of measles in this community, that's a serious issue."

Many of the problems now being experienced by television stations in Los Angeles may be directly attributable to the lack of foresight by previous managements. Instead of investing profits locally, the money was taken out of the community to other network stations. "Los Angeles," explained Huerta, "has subsidized other developing stations. The profits were continually being drained out."

Among the things the Los Angeles Spanish-language media could do better:

* **They could provide more coverage of neighborhood issues.** While Spanish-language media in this town are proficient enough to cover general local issues well, they must also learn to report the barrio news -- news that is too often ignored by everybody but is very important in the community. Stories about the nurse commended for her volunteer work, about the local businessman opening his third restaurant, about the migrant worker's child accepted by Harvard.

Jose Lozano, publisher of La Opinion, said his newspaper has been doing more of this, but must balance resources, time, and space. "These type of stories are vital to us," he said. "But we depend a lot on telephone tips to develop them."

Fernando Lopez, subdirector of news for Univision's KMEX, expressed the same concerns over the delicate balancing act. He has a 25-member news staff and one live news truck to produce two daily news shows Monday through Friday. (There are plans for a weekend news program.) The average English-language station may have a 150-member news staff to cover the Los Angeles area.

"Our resources are small in comparison and yes, there are a lot of things we would like to cover. Some days we do a good job. Other days we know we've missed stories. We're our own worst critics," Lopez said.

Arturo Gonzalez, radio news director, concurs. He has a four-member news staff for the AM-FM combo KTNQ/KLVE. "Our biggest problem is covering news with the reporters we have," he said. "We know we have to improve. We need to do it in more detail. We need to be less rushed and devote more time to it."

* **The media should provide more cultural programming.** Some view education of the masses as part of the media's responsibility. And without public stations in Spanish, existing stations must take on that role.

KMEX's Lopez said his station's news show does cover entertainment and the arts, but not extensively. "That will change as we develop and grow."

Cultural programming, too, will eventually find a niche in broadcasting when producers find a way of providing a quality show at a reasonable cost. "This is like any business," he added. "There is always talk of money and how to pay the bills. It comes down to how much it will cost. I think that cultural programming, if done right, can bring the ratings. It's a matter of time."

In La Opinion, Lozano had plans to resurrect a special arts-and-entertainment supplement by the end of 1989. The Sunday section, "La Comunidad," had previously been published weekly but was not self-supporting. The new format will be monthly. "We decided to bring it back because of reader response," Lozano explained.

* **The media should play a more active advocacy role on issues that are not always considered "traditional" Latino issues, such as education, trade, and the economy.** Some leaders said they wanted their media to "take the lead" much as the <u>Times</u> or as a network does. They believed Latino media, particularly those in Los Angeles, could be recognized as speaking for a large segment of U.S. Hispanics.

"Journalistically speaking maybe they're just here to report the facts, ma'am," conceded Romero, "but the media that serve an underclass need to do more. Their responsibility is different."

Media executives say they are playing more active roles. In the first few months of 1989, KTNQ had done three specials, including one on the California death penalty and another on Hispanic Vietnam veterans. "I think we will do more as necessity and demand increases," Gonzalez said.

* **The media should improve use of the language and require higher journalistic standards from staff members.** "Too often you see misspellings and grammatical mistakes," said Scarlata. "You hear Anglicized Spanish. I wonder if the journalist has gone to school. On one occasion, a weekly newspaper took one of my press releases, didn't touch a word, and a reporter put his name on it. I can't image anybody doing that, but it happened."

V. New York

The Market

True to its fame as a cosmopolitan city, New York has one of the most diverse Hispanic populations in the country. It is second only to Los Angeles as the largest Hispanic market. According to Strategy Research Corporation's 1989 study of the city, there are just over 2.7 million Hispanics in the 28-county New York area (which includes parts of New Jersey and Connecticut). They make up 13.1 percent of the total population, with a buying power of $18.9 billion -- the 1987 GNP for Chile. Two-thirds of the Hispanic population resides within the five New York City boroughs, with the Bronx and Brooklyn accounting for the greatest percentage of Hispanics. Puerto Ricans make up most of that population.

The average age for New York's Hispanics is 27.8 years, compared to 36.8 years for non-Hispanics. And the average annual household income is $26,121, considerably lower than the $39,662 for non-Hispanics.

Spanish continued to be the language of preference at home and social functions. At work, using both Spanish and English, or only Spanish, was preferred. Ninety-eight percent of those in Strategy Research focus groups said they like to listen to Latin music, which bodes well not only for radio stations, but for any Hispanic medium which emphasizes native culture.(1)

The Media

There are two Spanish-language dailies, El Diario/La Prensa and Noticias del Mundo. A third, El Vocero, is published in Puerto Rico and distributes a New York edition. There are also several weeklies. El Diario is clearly the oldest and most read of the newspapers. In 1989, El Diario's owner, Gannett Co., Inc., sold the newspaper to a local partnership, El Diario Associates, that includes publisher Carlos Ramirez. The change in ownership is important in many ways. First, it was seen as a positive move that would enable El Diario to act more freely to attract both new and old readers. The newspaper was expected to conduct its first market and readership survey. However, it also meant that Gannett, which had bought El Diario to create a national Spanish newspaper, had abandoned that idea as unworkable.

At the time of this writing, there was also talk of a second Spanish-language FM radio station that would compete with Spanish Broadcasting System's WSKQ-FM. AM stations include WADO, WJIT, and WKDM.

WNJU-TV (Channel 47) is the Telemundo station in New York, as well as the ratings leader. WXTV-TV (Channel 41) is the Univision affiliate.

The Power

The influence wielded by Hispanic media in New York varies depending on the issue, the audience, and, perhaps more important, who judges the effects. Most of the politicians, community leaders, and others interviewed for this book, however, agreed on one point: For good or bad, in sickness or in health, those who are most easily influenced by the Hispanic media are those who are most dependent on them.

Guillermo Linares is the president of the Asociacion Comunal de Dominicanos Progresistas, a grassroots community organization in the predominantly Dominican neighborhood of Upper Manhattan. Many of those he knows -- neighbors, families, and friends -- are recent arrivals from the Dominican Republic. "Among immigrant families who are new, the tendency is to rely almost entirely on the Hispanic media. Press first, then radio. This is how they get their basic information that is critical for their day-to-day survival. They have no other alternatives. So they form their impressions of what is around them through the newspaper or the radio station." This dependency worries Linares and others, who fear that the narrow focus of these media, in addition to their lack of quality and perspective, hurts the people who need help most. Spanish-dependent immigrants who need explanations, acculturation, and information, do not have the media alternatives bilingual Hispanics do.

"In the case of acute need for information," said John Downing, a communications professor at Hunter College who has written about ethnic media, "you cannot find it in these media. And that's a pity."

However, the recent immigrant is by no means the media's sole audience. Hispanics who have been in this country for years also read, listen, and watch. And politicians admit they read El Diario/La Prensa and Noticias del Mundo, and keep tabs on the broadcast stations, to feel the pulse of a population growing in numbers and political power.

"They (the Spanish-language media) influence politicians of all ethnic groups," admitted Amalia Betanzos, the only Hispanic on New York's Central Board of Education. "I think they look carefully at what the media are saying -- to a certain degree, of course. There's no structure in New York City -- outside the Catholic Church, and maybe not even that -- that can tell people what to do and they'll follow."

Betanzos was appointed to the Board of Education after an intense campaign by the media to appoint an Hispanic to a board that had none. "The fact that the media played up the issue of no Hispanic on the board made it all possible," she added.

Former mayor Koch's Hispanic Affairs adviser Luis Miranda said editorials influence city government "a fair amount" if written well and factually. "They can affect certain city procedures. The powers that be look at editorials to see if they are giving possible solutions. I know my office looks at editorials very carefully and I advise the mayor, particularly on Hispanic issues," he added.

But it isn't just the mayor's office where media have an impact. The death of a Dominican man at the hands of New York police sparked several stories in the media, leaders said, and prompted a thorough investigation by the department which resulted in the arrest of two officers.

Says Bronx Borough President Fernando Ferrer: "You can bet that every decision maker in this state reads every editorial page of every major newspaper. I do. You want to know what opinion molders are thinking and you want to see to what extent news coverage affects editorials and vice versa. With the Spanish-language media, the editorial page is a reflection of something extra, something special. Unlike the Daily News, Spanish-language media don't seek to be all things to all people. They speak to a specific segment of the community."

For politicians, Hispanic media provide a window into a community of potential voters. Whether these newspapers and stations truly represent Mr. and Mrs. Hispanic does not seem to matter, as long as politicians begging for votes perceive that they do. Many New York City and State elected officials have Hispanic staff members who translate stories in the media.

"Every day the mayor asks me what has been in the media," Miranda said. "We read every single article and I send him summaries of what the media say about issues. It's very important. I talk to him every single day about them."

Perhaps as important, Hispanic media are a vital part of any information campaign. One can reach Spanish-dependent recent immigrants only through these media. "From an activist's point of view, the Spanish-language media are really crucial in reaching a segment of our community," said Richie Perez, who heads Community Services Society.

The Society is a nonprofit, private social welfare agency more than 100 years old.

"That sector is primarily an older sector that tends to be not as acculturated into New York life," he added. "If we want to reach Puerto Ricans in their forties, fifties, working class folks, we need El Diario. If we don't use it, we miss a large group of the population that doesn't read Newsday, that doesn't pick up the Daily News."

Hispanic media are essential in political campaigns. Candidates purchase advertisements not as a token gesture, but as a sincere (if not desperate) search for the Hispanic vote. As a matter of fact, the influence of Hispanic media in City Hall or state government may not be felt as strongly as during campaign time.

"The politicians go after the endorsements," Betanzos said. "There's a general feeling that an editorial endorsement may translate into more coverage, possibly more sympathetic coverage. Politicians push hard to get their paid messages across, too, and on peak times -- during and after telenovelas (prime time soaps)."

A perfect example of this was former mayor Edward Koch's courting of the Hispanic media during the 1989 election. In the Summer of 1988, when polls reported his standing had dropped among Latino voters, he turned to three Spanish-language radio programs to promote his point of view. These were "Amorosamente" on WJIT, "WADO a Tu Lado" on WADO, and "Cita con El Alcalde" on WSKQ. The results were visible. Letters from Hispanic constituents increased from 10 per week to 75. Most cite the radio shows. Koch even learned to master a compliment to those who praised his work, by saying in accented Spanish, "Te amo" ("I love you").

"We use radio because of its interactive quality. You send a message and people are a phone call away," Miranda said.

Ferrer of the Bronx, the highest ranking elected Hispanic official in the city, writes a weekly column for El Diario and another for Noticias del Mundo. He considers both to be an important way of communicating with his constituents. "I think we use one another in a positive way. They have an impact on me, and I believe I have an impact on their reporting, if I do things that are newsworthy."

Not all readers, however, agree with the assessment that Spanish-language media serve as a catalyst for change. Ramon Morales, a businessman who owns Intelligent Technologies Corp., a data communications company in Manhattan, expressed grave doubts about the media's ability to influence policy. A consumer of both Spanish- and English-language media, he considers much of the Hispanic print and broadcast coverage to be frivolous and unprofessional.

"By and large, the Hispanic media in the city are irrelevant to the experience of the majority of Hispanic people. Very few stories that are aired will lead to several thousand Hispanics sending letters to City Hall," he said.

This, he added, can be attributed to the fact that "Spanish-language media completely forsake the younger Latino," who is bilingual and perhaps more attuned to the American way of forcing change. Furthermore, Morales worries that politicians wrongly view the Hispanic media as representative of Latino voices and values. "There is a wealth of thinking out there that is not reflected or captured or harnessed by the media. To read the newspapers, you would only get one viewpoint," Morales said.

If power is measured by the end result -- policy change, mobilization of a community, creation of leaders, legitimizing a hitherto unknown grassroots movement -- New York Hispanic newspapers qualify as the medium of record. El Diario, and to a lesser extent Noticias del Mundo, set the pace for what others will cover and, in some cases, what their Hispanic broadcast competition will say. The two dailies cannot compete with television (such as Telemundo's Channel 47) for audience reach, but the newspapers are devoted primarily to news, their efforts concentrated.

"Newspapers are the most influential in getting people to change," Linares said. "They tend to be accessible. They can be reproduced easily and they can be translated. The stories are longer and have more facts. They can create impact in a sustained way."

Julia Rivera is executive director of Aspira Association, Inc., of New York, a private educational and leadership development agency founded in 1961 by a group of Puerto Rican educators and professionals. She has been reading the New York Spanish-language dailies for several years and believes, as others do, that their influence within City Hall and among the community is growing. "In the last five years," she said, "I've seen more letters to the editors. That's a signal that people are reading them, reacting to them, thinking about them -- and maybe not liking them."

The sustained and concentrated effort Linares describes when speaking of newspapers is somewhat diluted in a medium such as radio or television where the bulk of the programming is entertainment. Though all New York Hispanic broadcast stations have talk shows about community events, too many are at odd hours when the audience tends to be quite small. Yet, because radio and television are so pervasive, broadcasting is an important part of any type of campaign. Neither medium, however, could force change alone.

Radio is of special importance in New York when trying to reach young Hispanics. As a matter of fact, some community leaders believe it is the only Spanish-language medium that reaches young Hispanics. Diana Caballero, director of the Puerto Rican/Latino Education Roundtable (an advocacy coalition), says radio has "a dedicated audience."

Once hooked on the music, they will tune in for the news and perhaps other shows. However, such impact is limited.

"Most of the young bilinguals," she adds, "read the Daily News. The 18-to-34-year-olds rely on television's 'Eyewitness News.' That age group doesn't read El Diario or Noticias."

The Impact

Media exercise their power in different ways. In New York, perhaps the most common is by creating leaders -- or at least creating the perception that a particular person quoted repeatedly has an original idea, expertise, or sound solutions to a problem. "The simple act of choosing whom to quote is power," said Caballero. "Newspapers pretty much set the agenda by what they report, how they report, and whom they quote. They not only can mold opinion but sometimes determine what direction an issue will take."

An example is the repeated interviews with Walter Alicea, president of the Hispanic Society of the New York police department. Once a relatively unknown officer, he emerged as a force in confrontations with Mayor Koch and the police commissioner over treatment of Hispanic police in early 1989, according to community activists. It is likely he would have been considered a leader among colleagues, but without the help of the media, others outside the police force would not have known about him.

But the power of creating leaders is not always used with discretion. Many of the younger community leaders complained that Hispanic media are not always accessible, that they too often take the easy way out by seeking only the "Old Guard" as sources, and ignoring the new wave of leaders.

"There's a whole new batch of young leaders who are not covered by the Hispanic media. They might not even know they're there. It might be because these leaders are more aggressive, and the media try to appeal to the middle class," said Morales.

Media also influence a community by legitimizing grassroots movements. It's like the proverbial trick question: If there was no one in the forest to hear the tree fall, did it make any noise? "Their coverage," explained Perez, the community activist, "validates us as a legitimate community-based effort. If you're not in the media, you don't exist. If your activity is not covered, it didn't take place."

El Diario's unflagging coverage of problems in the Hunts Point Peninsula in the Bronx, coupled with its editorials, was instrumental in forcing the government's hand. Stories criticized dilapidated housing, high crime, inadequate social services, and poor business development.

As a result, Bronx Borough President Ferrer established a task force in mid-1987. About 18 months later, the task force released a report stating that El Diario "helped prompt this effort with a series highlighting quality-of-life problems in Hunts Point."

Looking back at the stories, Ferrer admitted the newspaper played a vital journalistic role: "It struck a chord," he said. "It was influential in affecting governmental policy."

Newspaper endorsements can also, on occasion, influence government policy, but they do so very sporadically and indirectly at best. The hope of an endorsement can affect the way an incumbent official will react in a given situation. A false move could cost a politician the paper's approval; the right touch could tip the scales in his favor. There is widespread doubt, however, about the efficacy of an endorsement. Most people agree that it is a nice trophy to have, but does not truly affect the outcome of an election. Those who have made up their minds will vote for their candidate of choice no matter what the newspaper says. An endorsement may have some impact only on the small group of undecided voters. Morales cites the example of El Diario's endorsement of Herman Badillo's opponent in the comptroller's race several years ago. In spite of this, Badillo won an overwhelming percentage of the Hispanic vote. "Editorials," said Morales, "do not affect the vote to the extent editors and politicians believe."

The Problems

Complaints from readers and activists about Spanish-language media are very similar to those concerning mainstream media. In some cases, news executives would say it is not the media's purpose to be liked. Their function is to inform and entertain. However, the dissatisfaction voiced by those interviewed for this book was often well founded. Among the grievances:

* **Spanish-language media rarely scoop other media, even on Hispanic matters.** Only recently have the two Spanish dailies begun covering the Bronx as a full time beat. The borough has a 40-percent concentration of Latinos and the highest ranking elected Hispanic in the city.

The lack of aggressiveness by the media was one of the most repeated complaints. "You get no scoops. None, zero," Morales said. "They cover a story after it already has been covered."

Though limited by resources, media managers say such criticism is not always true or fair. "I like to think we're competitive," said Carlos Ramirez, publisher of El Diario. "It all depends on what you consider a scoop. We do come up first with stories that are important to our readers. Some of them are not followed by other media; some don't appear in other media until much later."

* **There are few news analyses and fewer investigative pieces.** There is no attempt to go beyond the surface of an event or an issue. "They're event oriented and crisis oriented and they don't go beyond that," said Diana Caballero.

Lamented Rivera of Aspira: "We have no Ted Koppels. We should have a show of his kind on Channel 41 or Channel 47. We need something that will do more than scan the surface and report the facts."

Rivera has several suggestions for stories that would be relevant to the community: what happens to the increasing number of Hispanic children in foster care; how Latinos deal with the taboo of placing an elderly relative in a nursing home; interracial marriages; the efficacy of care in hospitals where Spanish is not spoken. Though all are legitimate social concerns in the community, she doubts that they will be covered in a significant way by the media because they could be controversial and may take too much time and effort.

Helga Silva, news director of Telemundo's Channel 47, replies that Spanish-language media must deal with "enormous constraints in terms of personnel and other resources." Yet, her station has done specials on police brutality, women in jail, housing discrimination, sweat shops, unwed mothers, and other issues. This means she must pull one of her four reporters away from daily assignments.

"When I do this, I do it at a tremendous sacrifice," she explained. "It represents 25 percent of my reporting staff. You tell any newspaper or station, in English or in Spanish, to put 25 percent of its reporters on a story and you'll hear editors cry."

* **The quality of reporting is often lacking.** Activists say they find editing mistakes, factual errors, misleading information, and overall sloppy journalism. Rivera cites the example of El Diario/La Prensa's coverage of a "fight" between two community groups in the Bronx. The February 1989 story claimed one of those groups was the Fiesta Folklorica Puertorriquena Inc. The group had not held any events, and certainly had no disagreements, in the Bronx. In a strongly worded letter to the editor, the group's president wrote: "Neither the newspaper nor the reporter verified this information with us at any time."

"Instead of exposing just hearsay, they should come up with the facts," said Linares of Domincanos Progresistas. "One of the things the Village Voice does effectively is its homework. They back up what they say."

Ramirez said reporting problems are slowly being corrected, but that these are a function of inexperienced reporters and editors. One of the biggest problems El Diario faces, he added, is the turnover of talented staff as they move on to the Daily News or the Times.

"A newspaper is a rough draft of history, not the final word," he said. "We are guilty without question of sometimes distorting and fully reporting everything at that point in time. But we're also responsible and we come back and correct what we do wrong."

Media sometimes miss the story altogether, perhaps because of a lack of manpower. During the 25th anniversary of the Aspira Association in 1987, New York Governor Mario Cuomo came out publicly against the "English-only" movement for the first time. "None of our media attended," Caballero said. "They missed a good story."

By the same token, reporting has improved in recent years and activists do give the media credit for this. "Quality has improved," said Bronx Borough President Ferrer. "Compared to 20 years ago, it's night and day. Still, it's not where it should be."

* **The media lack vision, do not recognize trends, and function with typical knee-jerk reactions.**

From Caballero, the Puerto Rican educator: "They do not cover stories on a consistent basis and therefore cannot provide any perspective. Too often it is press-conference news, press-release rewrites."

Some media managers say such criticism is well founded, but they are making improvements. Said Elias Garay, news director of WSKQ-FM: "We are expanding, we are doing more local news, we are giving more emphasis to what our listeners want. But change sometimes comes slowly."

* **The media have not found a way to reach young Hispanics.** Morales calls these Latinos -- bilinguals who function in both languages and want news about Hispanic issues delivered in a professional way -- the "orphaned children" of the media. The Spanish-language press in particular has lost them to <u>Newsday</u> and the <u>Daily News</u>.

Others agree. "They would read if there were something there for them," Professor Downing said. "The fact is, there isn't."

* **Spanish-language newspapers and broadcast stations do not run enough "good stories" about Hispanic life in the United States.** They do not profile enough successful Latinos who could be displayed as role models. They do not run enough feature stories about immigrant families who have made it despite awesome odds. And they too often miss stories about activities that could do a community good. All of the leaders interviewed felt Hispanic media, as the voice of a minority, have a special role in this regard.

"Hispanic media," suggested school board member Betanzos, "should play more of an advocacy role. We have success stories, too."

VI. Miami

The Market

As the third-largest Hispanic market, the Miami area is home to more than one million Hispanics, with more than 90 percent of those living in Dade County, according to Strategy Research Corporation. The Hispanic growth rate in Dade County was a respectable 42 percent for the nine years ending in 1989. However, Broward County doubled its Hispanic population in that same period, to more than 91,000 people.

Hispanics make up 43 percent of Dade County's population, but only 7 percent of Broward's, and 15 percent of Monroe County, to the south of Dade. Compared to other Hispanic markets, Miami tends to be older and more retentive of the Spanish language. About 27 percent are under 18 years of age, and most are 35 and older. According to Strategy Research Corporation, 82 percent of Miami's Hispanics say Spanish is the principal language they speak.

Cubans are the dominant Hispanic nationality in the Miami area. They comprise 65 percent of Hispanic households, although the Central American population (17 percent) is growing rapidly, particularly the Nicaraguans.(1)

The Media

Miami has one of the healthiest Hispanic media markets in the country. In recent years, the city has been used more and more as a production center for news and talk show programs, mainly because Florida is not a union state and production costs are lower.

There are two Spanish-language dailies in Miami, Hispanic-owned Diario Las Americas and El Nuevo Herald, a Spanish-language edition of the Miami Herald. The latter paper was revamped in 1987 and given more editorial independence from its sister publication. Both its news staff and the space committed to news were doubled. It is now the largest Spanish-language newspaper in the Continental United States with a daily circulation of 98,000 and Sunday circulation of 111,000.

Univision's Channel 23 has long been a ratings leader and network innovator, but this station has seen some of its power erode vis a vis Telemundo's Channel 51.

Finally, radio plays a very important role in Miami's Hispanic community. There are two Spanish AM/FM combinations -- WQBA and WCMQ -- and five AM stations: WAQI, WOCN, WRHC, WSUA, and WWFE. The latter station went on the air in 1989. A third FM station, WTHM-Ritmo 98, is owned by Mambisa Corporation, the owner of WAQI.

In 1989, Mambisa and Heftel Broadcasting, owner of the Los Angeles AM/FM combo KLVE/KTNQ, announced that they planned to create a national Hispanic radio and print network named Viva America Media Group.

At the time of this writing, Tichenor Media System had reportedly bought WQBA -- the top-rated Spanish station in the market -- from Susquehana Broadcasting for more than $30 million. This would mean Tichenor now owns Hispanic stations in Texas, Chicago, and Miami.

The Power

Though among the youngest of Hispanic media, Miami's television, radio, and newspapers are probably the most influential in the country. This is because Miami Hispanics have a strong economic and political base with a high retention of language. Much of the influence has come about since the late 1970s, although Miami had a Spanish-language daily -- Diario Las Americas -- before the Cuban influx of the 1960s.

The role these media play is diverse, and depends greatly on ownership and format. By and large, the radio stations, particularly those with news/talk shows, are fervent advocates of Hispanic political issues, maninly anti-Communism. This is particularly true of Diario Las Americas. The two television stations and El Nuevo Herald tend to be more neutral, providing a more balanced reporting of events.

"They are," said Dade County school board member Rosa Castro Feinberg, "the town crier, the source of information on everything for Hispanics who are mostly Spanish-dependent. From our media, you can get advice from veterinarians, astrologers, priests, dentists, Social Security specialists. I think more importantly they are the place where political ideas are debated very vigorously and very extensively."

Because Miami is predominantly a community of political exiles -- both Cubans and Nicaraguans have fled Marxist regimes -- the media that serve them have strong political undertones. About half of Miami's radio stations, for example, have news/talk show formats that carry plenty of political news. In other markets, no station does. Furthermore, these more expensive news formats do very well. WQBA-AM has long been a ratings leader, though it is facing stronger competition from the FM music stations. Commentaries on these stations are often long and controversial; they air on prime time as well as repeatedly throughout the day.

By the same token, El Nuevo Herald's editorial pages, as well as Diario Las Americas', are followed closely by some Hispanics. The television stations, though mostly soaps and variety shows, also editorialize occasionally and have provided special news programs on a variety of subjects -- from hotly contested political races to hotly debated precepts of Santeria, a Caribbean religion which mixes African beliefs and elements of Catholicism.

Determining which medium -- print or broadcast -- is most influential in this community is particularly difficult because community leaders interviewed were divided in their assessment of influence and impact. There was no consensus on which -- radio, television, or newspaper -- exerted the more lasting, the most widespread change in attitude or behavior. There was, however, a general leaning toward the broadcast stations because of the far reach of television and radio.

Gonzalo Soruco, a professor at the University of Miami's School of Communication, conducted a survey of Dade Cubans' attitudes, preferences, and usage regarding available media. "Because of the power structure in Miami and the way media work," he explained, "I don't think we can pinpoint one medium as being more powerful. It depends more on the issue involved."

It also depends on the person making the judgment. Those who thought newspapers were the most influential cited El Nuevo Herald. Diario Las Americas, though well liked and a long-timer in the market, did not meet the quality and reporting standards leaders expected of it. It is popular with what many called the "Old Guard" -- mostly older, less acculturated Hispanics -- and its unaudited circulation of about 65,000 also limits the newspaper's reach. What's more, those we interviewed thought few events or issues reported in the paper had provoked reactions from leaders or readers.

El Nuevo Herald, on the other hand, has had a long antagonistic relationship with the Cuban community because it was viewed as a translated mouthpiece of the English-language Herald. Since the editorial and staff changes, including an office move away from corporate headquarters, the newspaper has garnered more favorable comments, even from its previously vociferous critics. "The relationship between the community and El Herald has changed a lot with El Nuevo Herald," said Miami Mayor Xavier Suarez. "I don't think it is as antagonistic as it once was."

However, because El Nuevo Herald is distributed as a supplement to the Miami Herald, and because the latter is not accepted by some Hispanics, there is a residual ill feeling toward the paper. Even with this, El Nuevo Herald often sets the agenda of what will be reported and what will serve as fodder for the talk shows and commentaries on the broadcast media. It is difficult for an Hispanic in Miami to avoid El Nuevo Herald, even if he or she does not read it. If a Latino listens to radio, he will likely hear something that appeared on the paper's front page, sometimes verbatim, sometimes with embellishments of a highly critical nature.

"Undoubtedly the financial condition of El Herald is so strong that it can provide the news coverage other stations cannot," said Osvaldo Soto, chairman of the Spanish American League Against Discrimination. "You go to any radio station in the morning and they have the Herald or El Herald, in English and Spanish. The main source of news is newspapers, and it determines what will be covered that day."

While a newspaper has the ability to cover many issues, radio and television reach a broader range of people. In many instances, Miami's news stations scoop the newspapers and provide repeated commentary on issues the papers may cover only in passing. This continual coverage and editorializing does have an impact on the community.

School board member Castro Feinberg believes radio sways the most people. During her political campaign as an underdog candidate, she spent her entire advertising budget on radio and bus benches. Bus benches, she said, were not particularly effective. Radio was.

"They serve as a catalyst for action," she said. "Why do you think that on election night the politicians make the rounds of the emisoras (stations)? If they spend so much time doing that, you know it must matter."

Television, others counter, is the strongest force. "You have to take into consideration their reach in the market," said Juan Garcia, a political consultant who was formerly chief aide to Mayor Suarez. "When they editorialize, it's pretty seldom. But when they do, I can tell you politicians do listen. An editorial on TV can destroy you. In the print media, the politicians can run a little scared."

Some believe Spanish-language newspapers, radio, and television stations are losing their audiences to Anglo counterparts. English-language television stations have mounted an all-out campaign to attract Latinos, and they are succeeding. Professor Soruco's study shows that the "preponderance of preference is for television -- and English-language television" among Cubans.

Lamented Garcia: "We've seen it (broadcast) getting weaker, although it is still necessary to reach a segment of our population. Ratings are down. Stations holding the market are the neutral ones, the music stations. Where we used to get seven points, we get four or five now. We used to get knockout soap operas. We no longer see that. The boom of Hispanic media in Miami was in the late 1970s. They were capturing the market that wasn't bilingual enough.

"Now we've been losing the market to the English media, even when we count the immigrants."

The Impact

Whether the loss of some of the Spanish-language media's audience is a permanent trend and how it translates into a loss of influence is unclear. In Miami, all media wield their power in a subtle, constant way, but some influence more persistently than others. As in other cities, they have been instrumental in providing a forum for emerging leaders and ideas. Without them, many Latino activists and grassroots groups would receive little press play. Nicaraguan banker Roberto Arguello said that when he and a group of countrymen were trying to organize the Nicaraguan-American Bankers Association, they sought the media to get the word out.

"Nobody paid attention to us until they started covering us," recalled Arguello. "Then people began to see us and we had politicians come to us. Without the media, you cannot exist. Or, it would be almost impossible."

Leslie Pantin, a past president of the Little Havana Kiwanis Club, which coordinates Calle Ocho Open House and other festivals during Miami's Carnaval, cited the Spanish-language media as being instrumental in the event's success.

"We asked people how they heard about Calle Ocho and they invariably said (Spanish) TV and radio and newspaper," he added.

The news media's repeated references to certain community figures imbue them with an aura of power and expertise. Arguello is often used as a Nicaraguan spokesman by the media. He is then perceived by others as such and what he says carries more weight.

Coverage and play of certain stories also helps gauge community interest. Aida Levitan, who ran for city commissioner, said the media serve as a barometer for leaders on all levels. "The more coverage an issue gets, the more it will be identified by politicians as a pressing issue," said Levitan, president of the public relations division of Sanchez & Levitan, Inc. "From my own experience I can tell you that opinion surveys conducted by Hispanic media are important to me in shaping my own opinions about what others consider important."

For better or worse, extensive stories and editorials sometimes make an issue bigger than it is. Yet, it is in these examples where one can measure a cause-and-effect action by the media. In 1984, when Jane Fonda was scheduled to appear at two department stores in Miami to promote a beauty product, several Spanish-language radio stations called on the community to boycott her visit. Commentators believed Fonda's actions during the Vietnam War were suspect and insulting, particularly to those who had fled Communist regimes. The stations mobilized the community in such a way, and the calls to the stores were such, that Fonda's visit was cancelled. In a similar case in 1986, media commentary on a playwright's dealings with the Cuban government resulted in the banning of that play from the Festival of Hispanic Theater.

In more recent years, however, the ability of the media -- primarily radio -- to mobilize the community has not been as effective. This may be a result of a changing community, less interested in the virulent anti-Castro rhetoric and more aware of pressing local concerns, or the fact that only some issues lend themselves to propagation. For example, at the time of this writing, Spanish-language media in Miami had been covering and providing extensive commentary on the deportation case of Orlando Bosch, a man considered a convicted terrorist by the U.S. government and a freedom fighter by some Cubans. Calls for hunger strikes, marches, and business shutdowns did not spark widespread interest or compliance.

Similarly, radio talk show hosts in the Summer of 1989 criticized Miami Mayor Suarez and Hispanic city commissioners for what one called "an act of treason." The commission had voted to appoint a black activist to a vacant seat until the November elections. Some members of the media considered it a Latin seat. Informal surveys by other media, however, showed that many Latinos did not consider it such a big issue, and about half had not even heard of the controversy.

"Sometimes," said Garcia, "they try to force the issue. I think the media are successful when they interpret the community's feelings."

In other words, the media may be influential only when their audience wants to be influenced.

The power to mobilize the community may rest as much in media personalities as in the media outlets themselves. Radio commentators especially have sometimes emerged as leaders and opinion molders in their own right. A classic example occurred during the 1988 federal prison riots by Cuban inmates. Tomas Garcia Fuste of top-rated WQBA-AM became a key liaison between prisoners and federal officials in Oakdale, Louisiana.

Whether the media serve as a catalyst for governmental change is more difficult to measure. Some leaders interviewed admitted they watched Spanish-language media, as well as English, and occasionally reacted to something read, watched, or heard there. Television's polling of political races, for instance, is something Mayor Suarez said he watches closely. (Both Channel 23 and 51 polls are widely quoted in other media.) School board member Castro Feinberg said she tunes in to the radio, particularly the talk shows. Because of a comment raised during one of these talk shows, Castro Feinberg introduced and helped pass through the school board a measure to create "safe zones" around schools. She also participates in a talk show on WQBA once each month.

Banker and activist Carlos Arboleya, on the other hand, said he is not swayed by the media. "I believe some people are easily influenced by the media and are scared of media pressure. I don't feel that way. I've had to swallow and stand up to media pressure," he said.

The Problems

Much of the criticism of Miami's Spanish-language media centers on their role as advocate and champion. Perhaps this role taken to an extreme can alienate the community if an outlet misreads the public's wishes. Several leaders interviewed cited what Professor Soruco so aptly called "a fixation on Castro," at the expense of other issues. That is not to say that the fight against the Cuban dictator, as well as the Nicaraguan leftist government, is not important to Miami's Hispanics. It is, but many want to see more -- more local news, more analysis of problems closer to home.

Among some of the criticisms:

* **The media in Miami tend to rest on their laurels and have not kept pace with a changing community.** "They are static," Garcia said, "but we're not." Radio must update formats; not necessarily change from news/talk to music, but cover more local issues. Diario Las Americas must modernize itself as well, in everything from reporting to layout. Clearly, some feel, the emphasis should shift away from the old Cuban rhetoric.

"The Spanish media in Miami are the only ones that are not considered liberal," countered Tomas Garcia Fuste, news executive at WQBA. "That is considered a problem to some. We have been very successful with our format. In Dade alone, we are the top rated of all stations. Why should we change? Our public supports us."

Alina Torres, news director at Univision's Channel 23, said the television station has made a conscious effort to evolve as the community has evolved. "We don't have the same format as the Spanish-language radio stations," she said. "We do not editorialize in our news stories."

* **The media should be more discriminating in whom they allow on the airwaves.** Though in theory the idea of open access sounds wonderful, leaders complained that the result is usually a mixture of inaccurate information and opinion.

"They need to be more responsible and careful not to spread rumors and misinformation," Levitan said. "There should be a conscious avoidance of demagoguery. Though this has changed somewhat, there was a period when people on the air would do anything for ratings."

* The media need to offer more and better coverage of business and economic issues -- such as real estate, banking, and finance. Many of those interviewed said they must get this information from the English-language media. Because so many of Miami's Hispanics are business people and merchants, they said they want this type of information tailored to their needs and in their language.

El Nuevo Herald editor Carlos Verdecia agrees that not enough is being done on this front. That may change, however. The paper is looking to add "Lunes Financiero," a financial tab, on Mondays. "Business coverage is something we do worry about. It is something we're looking at with great interest," he said.

Coverage in the electronic media may be more difficult to accomplish. Garcia Fuste of WQBA said business stories are covered as the need warrants; in television, the subject is not given a lot of play because it is so specialized.

"It's a valid concern," Torres said, "but to have a specialist cover those issues one has to have a larger staff. We try to do it as much as possible, but it's a matter of juggling reporters."

* The media need to focus on better coverage of other Hispanic groups in addition to the Cuban majority. While South Florida is becoming more Latin, it is also becoming less Cuban.(2) Statistics from the U.S. Census Bureau and the Dade County Planning Department show that the population of Central and South Americans is growing quickly, while Cuban growth has slowed to a trickle.

Though more and more outlets are covering these communities, it is still not enough; much of that coverage depends, unfortunately, on whether an outlet has a Colombian or Nicaraguan or Puerto Rican reporter. Survival of these media may very well depend on their ability to diversify.

Garcia Fuste disagrees with the assessment that there is not enough coverage of other groups. "I have just finished a week's programming on Colombia," he said. The station, he added, has also done several fundraisers for victims of catastrophes in other Latin American countries.

From Channel 23's Torres: "We have been very conscious of the opinions of our Cuban viewers, but we don't consider our audience to be only Cuban. We do a good number of Cuban stories, but we also do cover the other communities. We program for all Hispanics."

VII. San Antonio

The Market

San Antonio is the fourth-largest Hispanic market in the country, with an estimated 965,500 Hispanics -- almost half of the area's population. Growth among the Hispanic population in this area has been phenomenal. According to Strategy Research Corporation, Hispanics in the San Antonio ADI increased by 57 percent from 1980 to 1988.(1)

This, too, is a young market -- 41 percent of the Hispanics are under 18, and another 28 percent are between 18 and 34, according to Strategy Research Corporation. Most are of Mexican descent. Many have resided there for 30 years or more, which speaks strongly of the permanence and roots of that community. This is especially true when compared to Hispanics in Los Angeles (11 years, 9 months average residency); New York (13 years, 3 months); Miami (13 years); and Chicago (12 years).

The Media

San Antonio has no Spanish-language daily, although La Prensa, a promising weekly, had published a few issues at the time of this writing. The city has a healthy broadcast market. The oldest Spanish-language television station in the country was founded here -- Univision's KWEX Channel 41. Telemundo is also expected to enter the market.

Radio is thriving. KCOR-AM signed on as the first Spanish-language station in the United States in 1945. Other AM stations include KEDA, KRIA, and KSAH. The most exciting entry has been the switch into Spanish of an FM station, KZVE. All have musical formats with news broadcasts aired at least every hour.

The Power

Though Spanish-language media in San Antonio are among the oldest in the country, they are not among the most powerful. As a matter of fact, perhaps their very age, lack of competition, and complacency have prevented them from progressing as their audience might like. For example, the Univision station was the only game in town for many years, and the first Spanish outlet to go on the air in this country. Yet it was only in 1989, under new management, that it added an evening news program. It has no weekend program. The change, community leaders believe, was not initiated from within but as a reaction to Telemundo's proposed entry into the market.

Most radio stations have accepted their meager lot, and have not attempted to cover some of the serious issues facing San Antonio Hispanics in a responsible, comprehensive way. They have few prime-time talk shows and small news programs, with rare exceptions.

Furthermore, the power of the media in this city is also hampered by the lack of Spanish-language print. San Antonio has no daily newspaper targeted only to Hispanics. Because the print medium tends to be the strongest catalyst for change with its ability to provide a sustained, comprehensive look at problems, the voice of San Antonio media as a whole is weakened by this lack. In its stead, the two English-language dailies have tried to find their niche within the community.

"You'd be missing a big segment of the Hispanic community if you didn't use the Anglo media," explained Ramiro Cavazos, executive director of the Hispanic Chamber of Commerce in the city.

San Antonio may have the most acculturated Hispanics in the country. Many are second, third, and fourth generations, educated in English. They speak Spanish but do not always write or read it. Their ties are firmly set in Texas, particularly since many of them were raised in an environment where assimilation was essential to survival. In its 1989 U.S. Hispanic market study, Strategy Research Corporation found more widespread use of English among San Antonio Hispanics than in other large markets: 43 percent of San Antonio's Hispanics spoke their native tongue at home most frequently compared to 78 percent nationally, 75 percent in Los Angeles, and 82 percent in Miami.

There is no doubt that the power of the ethnic media depends not only on their constituencies' political and economic power, but also on language dependency and preference. If San Antonio Hispanics prefer English, if they have been educated in English, it is likely that they will be primarily English-media consumers.

"They consume Spanish media for music and entertainment, but not always for information," said Federico Subervi, a professor in the Department of Radio, Television, and Film at the University of Texas at Austin.

In research on Spanish-language media content in the 1984 presidential election, Subervi found that San Antonio radio stations provided basic coverage but no more than that. "They provided less than other cities in comparison," he explained. This limited coverage could be a result of managements' realization that area Hispanics were getting more and better information from their English-language counterparts. Or, in the proverbial dilemma of the chicken and the egg, maybe listeners tuned out the Spanish stations because these outlets did not provide the information they wanted.

That is not to say, however, that those who prefer English will not tune in to Spanish media if given a good reason. On the contrary. All elected officials and civic activists interviewed for this book complained that "their" local radio and television stations did not do enough to reach out to bilingual Hispanics. The media outlets preferred to cater only to recent immigrants or an older generation. Thus, they left the bilingual Hispanic with little choice but to consume Anglo media. Though there has been a gradual turning away from this concept (the entrance of the new FM station into the market and changes within the Univision station), San Antonio's media are losing a potential market -- perhaps their most important market -- by not capturing the bilingual, bicultural Hispanic.

Raquel Oliva, a businesswoman and community leader, explains it this way: "I can reach more Hispanics, especially those with influence, through the English media. If I'm on Spanish, I'm reaching a small, select population."

Democratic State Rep. Dan Morales says Spanish-language media are most influential with the 30-and-over generation. "My parents and grandparents listen and watch. The young ones are primarily English-language consumers."

There are cross-over media consumers, those who use media in both Spanish and English. This tends to happen on what Subervi calls an "issue specific" basis. In other words, San Antonio Hispanics use English-language media for their daily information needs. But when they are interested in a specific Hispanic issue or candidate, they tune in to both the English and Spanish media.

Spanish-language media do play an important informational role in the lives of Spanish-dependent San Antonians. Without radio and television stations, community leaders say, they would not be able to get information to this select part of the community. "When I need to get information to the people, I must use Spanish-language radio," said Councilwoman Maria Berriozabal, whose district is predominately Hispanic. "That is an important part of any campaign."

Providing basic information is what radio and television stations in San Antonio do best. For example, Oliva reported that publicity of events by the media usually results in a good turnout for the Woodlawn

Lake Community Association, a group started in 1982 by residents of one of the oldest San Antonio neighborhoods.

Cavazos said that the Hispanic Chamber's two television programs -- a monthly show for announcements and a weekly covering topical issues -- keep Hispanics up to date in a unique way. But the media do not venture beyond the simplicity of that informational role, be it because of lack of resources or apathy.

"The media, in general, don't take active stands on issues, but they're good at providing access to reach the community," Cavazos explained.

Said Berriozabal: "What I hear on Spanish-language newscasts is more a product of our collective actions, than information that would make me act. They're reactive, not proactive."

The ability to influence is evenly divided between radio and television in this city, with particular programs or stations being cited as those with the power to mobilize the community, or spark change within the status quo. Primarily, these are KCOR-AM's news program and KWEX Channel 41's public-service shows. However, San Antonians interviewed for this book were hard pressed to name one outlet that consistently delivered what they expected in a very basic sense. Even outlets with news staffs did not have the wherewithal to cover events on weekends, let alone provide some analysis on the issues of the day.

"They're very limited in what they can do," Oliva said. "Weekend crews are nonexistent, yet so many of our activities happen on weekends."

The Impact

The limited power wielded rests in the hands of media personalities and depends on the issue. In other words, sometimes broadcasters pick certain issues to serve as banners of civic consciousness. These issues include immigration, bilingualism, and voter registration. The media also are powerful enough to motivate people to contribute money and goods to various fundraising telethons, which leaders point out are vital as a unifying force within the community.

"They're very, very good in raising funds for people in distress," said Shirl Thomas, assistant to the San Antonio mayor and council. "In that way, I think they play an important humanitarian role you might not see from other stations."

They also exercise some influence by simply providing a forum for political leaders. Councilwoman Berriozabal, for example, was the only Hispanic official opposed to a domed city stadium. She could not find an English-language medium that would present her views as the hotly contested issue evolved in early 1989. However, when Channel 41 sponsored a debate, the station invited her and presented what she believed was a fairer picture. State Rep. Morales also cited Channel 41 and KCOR-AM for their coverage on bond issues for the construction of schools. The TV station has handled some tough issues as well, such as crime and child abuse.

The same accessibility is true for Hispanic issues that might not be covered by mainstream media. The Spanish-language media's initial coverage of the deterioration of the Woodlawn Lake neighborhood helped focus attention on the problem. Oliva, who helped found the community association, credits radio and television for helping to bring about change, including community pride and renewed interest in the area.

"The media can be influential. They can give importance to what you are doing. If they cover you over and over again, people know about you. They somehow make you more worthwhile and important," Oliva said.

Said Morales: "By virtue of their selection of guests and how they deal with an issue, they play an important role in the community. They can have an impact politically and philosophically to a certain extent by simply performing as news media."

The Spanish-language media also have served as liaison between government and the community. Lionel Sosa, president of Sosa & Associates, an advertising agency, cited the media's support and continual coverage of the San Antonio Education Partnership for the program's success. The partnership -- implemented to fight the high dropout rate, especially among Hispanics -- brings together schools, businesses, and colleges to promise a job or education to high school students who maintain a B average and a 95-percent attendance record. In less than one year, the number of students who met those requirements rose from 17 percent to 59 percent.

Several years ago, the media also criticized the city administration for hiring a city attorney who was not Hispanic. The city attorney at the time of this writing is Hispanic. Thomas, the assistant to the mayor, believes that media attention may eventually have led to action.

Yet, such examples of influence in effecting change are rare. What's more, measurable results or policy changes have come about only in conjunction with coverage by mainstream media. That is to say, Spanish-language media spark the interest and cover the first stories, but it is the mainstream press and broadcast stations that bring it to the attention of those in power. Many expressed doubt that elected officials, even those who understood Spanish, listened or watched Spanish-language media.

Morales said he did pay attention to Spanish-language media. "If there's a problem in my district, certainly I listen to them," he said. He admitted, though, to using more English-language media because they tend to be more comprehensive.

The Problems

The most oft-heard complaint about the media is their lack of analytical, explanatory, or investigative journalism. "They use our press releases word for word," one leader after another told me. This practice, instead of pleasing them, inspired a certain apprehension that most outlets are not being as discriminating as they should in what they communicate to the audience.

While most stations are conscientious about covering news conferences, filming openings of special programs, and airing public-service announcements, they do not offer in-depth looks at the problems of the high school dropout rate, housing, job discrimination, and issues of more pressing concern.

"A lot of times they just cover the hype, the attention-getting news," lamented Oliva. "They cover the news of the day and don't go beyond, into the heavy issues. They're skimming over what's happening."

Other complaints include:

* **The media lack original reporting.** Leonard Anguiano, director of special programs for the Mexican-American Cultural Center, said San Antonio's Spanish-language media are "so entertainment driven" that they tend to lose sight of their other informational function -- providing news. When they do provide it, too much of the focus can be on international news instead of local.

"The media are very important to us," he added. "They serve as documents, as a story of people's involvement in social activity. For that, they need to focus on issues."

There have been instances of good, original coverage. In 1989, for example, Channel 41 and KCOR provided excellent coverage of the pursuit and consequent killing of a satanic cult leader in a nearby town. In some instances, they scooped mainstream media.

Ramiro Cordoba, news director of KCOR, said its daily news coverage is the best of the local Hispanic radio stations. "With six members on the news staff, we can send a reporter but the others must use the teletype," he said.

Limited resources, however, do hurt coverage. "The budget has a lot to do with how and what we cover," he added. "If we don't have the manpower, that's all we can do."

* **Reporting, community leaders say, is not always accurate.** This problem, they add, stems from a lack of resources. Spanish-language media reporters must often cover several stories in one day, which opens the door to sloppy reporting. "They rarely get information

totally right," sighed Oliva. "When they do get it straight, I'm thrilled."

Josie Goytisolo, director of programming, news, and public affairs, said coverage by Channel 41 has been improving steadily. By 1989, after 18 months at her job, she had added an evening news program, hired an assignment editor, begun a video library, and hired more staff. The news budget increased by 70 percent, although she considered it to be at 1985 levels. With four reporters and six cameras, she felt she "could see the light at the end of the tunnel" but was not near her goal.

"In all fairness, I believe we have been improving and doing better. But yes, we don't have beat reporters. They're pulled away two or three times to do stories. My goal is to continue establishing credibility. More awareness and credibility will generate more money for the station. That in turn will prove that we can make money," she said.

* **Staff and programs are not reflective of the community.** "They don't use local talent," said Berriozabal. "They import it."

Goytisolo, who is Cuban, admitted that it was difficult being accepted in the predominantly Mexican-American community. But, she countered, she did not hire any Cubans for the staff.

"There was no need to. I found the talent right here. We have good, young reporters. One of them is going to 'TV Mujer' (a network show)," she said. "The reality is Mexican-American. At the same time, I want to be judged as a professional, not as a Cuban."

VIII. Chicago

The Market

As the sixth-largest Hispanic market, the Chicago area has 870,800 Latinos -- a growth of 17 percent between 1985 and 1989, according to Strategy Research Corporation. Most of these live within Cook, Kane, and Lake counties.

It is a young population: 40 percent are under 18 and 74 percent are under 35. It also may be among the most diverse of the Hispanic markets. Mexicans are the leading group, making up 43 percent of the population, but Puerto Ricans make up 28 percent; there are also sizable Central and South American and Cuban communities.

Strategy Research Corporation reports that 72 percent of Chicago's Hispanics use Spanish most frequently at home, and another 23 percent speak both languages at home.(1)

The Media

The biggest news of 1989 was the swap in network affiliations between the two independently owned Spanish-language television stations in Chicago. When the dust cleared, it appeared Univision had lost the battle and Telemundo had won a sizable market. However, the results are still out, and it promises to be an interesting race. Chicago may be the sixth-largest Hispanic market, but it happens to be the third-largest television market. Both sides agree that it is underexploited.

This is what happened: In October 1988, Univision and WSNS (Channel 44) announced the ending of their contract which had lasted well over three years. Reasons for the breakup were vague, but the Chicago

Tribune reported that WSNS had requested financial considerations which Univision found unacceptable. WSNS then signed with Telemundo. On a different front, the contract between WCIU (Channel 26) and Telemundo was about to expire. Univision quickly signed an affiliation agreement with the station.

The switch in network affiliations means several things for the Chicago television market: First, WCIU, which used to carry Hispanic programming part-time, in the late afternoon, gained more national advertising dollars and local ad money because of top-rated Univision shows. At the same time, Telemundo won over a full-time Spanish-language affiliate, not just a five-nights-a-week deal. However, WSNS, which first came on the air in 1985, probably lost the prestige and dollars attached to Univision programming. On both counts, however, the viewer won. Competition for viewers will continue to increase, translating into better programming, and improved news shows. The number of programming hours per week of Spanish-language television in this market has been increasing steadily -- from 30 hours in 1962 to 168 hours in 1989. Viewers can expect more and better.

There are three full-time Spanish-language radio stations in Chicago -- WOJO and WIND owned by Tichenor Media System, and WTAQ. A fourth was expected to go on the air at the time of this writing. There are at least two part-time Spanish-language stations too.

The print media are, without a doubt, the most numerous. A dozen or more newspapers are scattered around the neighborhoods of Chicago, but few, if any, have a citywide circulation. One or two may claim to be dailies, but readers and activists say regular publication and wide distribution is neither frequent nor expected.

Compared to their counterparts in other Hispanic markets, the Chicago Spanish-language media are very young and at the very early stages of development. "We are the new kid on the block," said Zeke Montes, publisher of _Tele Guia_ and former president of the National Association of Hispanic Publications. "In other Hispanic cities, the media have a history."

The Power

The power of Hispanic media in Chicago is muted. Sometimes their collective voice is silent. As a matter of fact, in no other city was the consensus so clear: Spanish-language media here do not usually influence politicians or mobilize the community. However, this is not as dismal as it sounds. The power of the media emerges with their growth; it is an integral part of their development. And because Chicago Latino media are so young, their impact has yet to be felt.

"In Chicago," said Esther Nieves, who was executive director of the Mayor's Advisory Commission on Latino Affairs in early 1989, "the influence of the Latino media is relatively new in that more local/community weeklies have appeared in the past four or five years. It's more of an informational media at this point, than a crusading media."

Though growing and improving, the city's media cannot always be depended on as a tool to reach Hispanics, particularly the growing bilingual segment. Their counterparts in the English-language media are still essential to get the message to the barrios. This could be either a sign of significant acculturation -- or the failure of Latino media to reach a potential audience.

Arturo Jauregui is the staff attorney for the Chicago office of the Mexican-American Legal Defense and Educational Fund (MALDEF). As a civil rights organization, MALDEF considers media coverage essential to its crusades. But he admits he needs the Anglo media more than the Latino. After the passage of the 1988 immigration law, MALDEF began an aggressive campaign to inform people about possible discrimination. Jauregui said the organization placed ads in Spanish newspapers, television, and radio stations. The few calls the ads elicited on such a controversial topic disappointed Jauregui.

"If we've just filed a suit against the State of Illinois on behalf of Hispanics, we have to make sure we get it in the Tribune and the Sun-Times. In the Hispanic media, yes, they would be outraged, but we don't have the political muscle necessary to implement change yet. We have to resort to the public at large. Politicians may be offended by a newspaper article, for example, but they will analyze it: How many people are going to read this, what can they do to me, how can they hurt me? If they find it's not much, then it's not going to matter."

As an information source for new immigrants who are monolingual, Spanish-language media remain an essential tool. Graciela Kenig, who served as director of communications for the Latino Institute in early 1989, makes sure even the smallest publication receives information about an upcoming event in order to attract people, especially if she aims for the less acculturated segment.

The media's success in drawing people to an event, though, does not translate into the media's ability to spark change. "When I've seen measurable change," she added, "it's because the Latin community itself has made enough noise and the mainstream media have covered it."

In a study commissioned by Peoples Gas, the majority of the Hispanic leaders interviewed watched both Spanish- and English-language TV but tended to watch English more than Spanish. They also tended to depend more on the English radio stations though they listened to both. Furthermore, Chicago's two major daily newspapers had a larger readership than the Spanish community newspapers, as expected. However, almost nine of every ten leaders interviewed read a Spanish-language newspaper. These figures on media preferences support Jauregui's theory: Spanish-language media are used, but not as much as possible.

Edward Villarreal, a former news executive of a Spanish-language television station, says the relationship between Chicago Hispanic media and audience is passive. "It's a source of information and entertainment and nothing more," said Villarreal, who now is operations manager of the Fox television station in the city. "As far as advocacy of issues, there are few instances of editorial lines."

Yet, the influence of Chicago's Latino media may not be defined as traditionally as in other markets because of the nascent stage of their development, said Professor Ilya Adler. Take this theory a step further to his conclusion: The media will wield considerable influence as they grow and improve, and as their audience gains political power.

Adler hosted a radio program and edited a bilingual weekly in California in the 1960s. As a professor in the Department of Communication and Theater at the University of Illinois at Chicago, he has researched the Latino media for several years. He believes that while not powerful or noticeably influential now, Spanish-language media have been very important in the political process of Latinos in Chicago thus far.

"They have made it possible for Latino politicians to communicate with Latino people. The media have given them an arena, and, let's face it, it's difficult to establish leadership without a public arena," he said.

Without Spanish-language media, Hispanic leaders would not have been able to present themselves as such to their constituents and certainly not to the rest of society. "The role of Latino media in Chicago," Adler added, "has been to give the community a stronger, unifying voice that has made Latinos realize there are others who share the same concerns. That, in turn, can trigger political action."

As in other Hispanic markets with a poorly developed print medium, activists gave credit to radio as the medium with the most impact. In fact, the Peoples Gas study of Hispanic leaders found that Spanish-language radio reaches more of them than Spanish-language television. "Radio," says Jauregui of MALDEF, "is everywhere. Anywhere you go into a Mexican community, any Mexican establishment, the radio is on. You are completely bombarded."

This is true not only of Mexican-Americans. Prof. Adler calls Latinos "radio addicts" and Chicago "a true radio city." Part of this Hispanic favoritism may be cultural.

"Latinos have always been big radio listeners, here and in their countries. It's an older medium, too. It's been here longer than television and it will also reach bilinguals who might see Anglo television and read English newspapers but still tune in for Latin music," Adler added.

However, music is not the only cultural reinforcement they provide. Talk shows such as "Todo un Poce," "La Voz del Pueblo," "Enfoque," "Desayunando con Fernando Fernandez," and others have helped to bring issues and new leaders into the forefront of public attention.

"AIDS is a good example," Adler said. "While mainstream radio will talk about it at midnight, Spanish-language radio has addressed it on prime time and very straight on. It's much more educationally oriented."

But some doubt that radio has the type of influence that can bring about change in behavior. It can inform, yes, discuss issues, and provide leaders with a forum but not serve as a catalyst -- yet. "You don't have the ability of Spanish-language radio to mobilize the community," said Dr. Luis M. Salces, senior vice president of Unimar advertising agency and a sociologist. "It does not yet have a history of activists and movements as black radio does in Chicago."

If a Chicago Spanish-language medium is to emerge as a political force, the safe money would go to a broadcast outlet. Though there are dozens of newspapers, none has emerged as a quality product with distribution in many neighborhoods. "My experience has been that newspapers don't have too much impact," Kenig said. "They're too fragmented."

And their quality is poor. "They leave much to be desired," complained Adler. "Important breakthrough stories -- stories that make waves -- usually come from print. But print in Chicago is not developed to that extent."

Neither is television, mainly because Channels 44 and 26 are relatively young and are just now recovering from a switch in networks. However, weigh them in as contenders if management decides to spend money to improve news and community programming.

"TV changed drastically when Univision came in two years ago," said Marta Ayala, director of program services for the Mayor's Advisory Commission on Latino Affairs. "Competition always improves quality. I think we could use more shows like 'Mesa Redonda' and 'Ayuda.' There's never enough of that."

The Impact

On the rare occasions that Spanish-language media have flexed their muscle in this city, leaders have applauded. In 1988, for example, Channel 44 did a series of stories on immigration that impressed several of the people interviewed. Channel 26 focused a series on education and overcrowded schools. Esther Nieves, of the Mayor's Advisory Commission on Latino Affairs, said the press -- including Anglo media -- played an important role in stirring up the ire of the community when her group issued a controversial report on health services for Latinos. The report called for hiring more Hispanics in top levels of the Health Department and the allocation of more funds to fight AIDS, improve mental health, and reduce infant mortality among Hispanics. The results were felt: In December 1988, the Chicago Health Commissioner promised to hire more Hispanic employees and earmark one-third of the department's budget to fight AIDS in the Hispanic community.

The media have crusaded particularly well on what activists call "safe issues" -- immigration, bilingual education, and voter registration. The overwhelming majority of Hispanics agree on such issues, so the media do not run the danger of alienating an audience or potential advertisers.

"They are still timid," said Adler. "They are not willing to shock. Daring they are not. They're very, very conservative and react, as expected, as a business. They simply aren't willing to rock the boat."

Despite audience criticism of the media, politicians and their aides say they do watch, listen, and read them regularly. It is their way of gauging community interest in a particular issue.

Alderman Jesus Garcia represents an electoral district that is 85 percent Latino, most of it Mexican. He is a Spanish-media consumer who uses them as a barometer of community interest in issues.

"A lot of stories," he said, "help me to prioritize some of the goals. You realize what people out there perceive as the burning issues of the day."

Media's influence, however, is limited because of the scope of their coverage. "You just don't see a whole lot of investigative journalism or in-depth, analytical stories," Garcia added.

In the simplest sense, media help to create leaders, as Adler suggested, by providing them with a forum. If a community activist is not annointed by the press or the broadcast stations, it is likely that his organization will not receive the support needed. "When there's an issue," explained Jauregui, "the media tend to automatically contact certain people and these people are projected as leaders."

But these people may or may not be true leaders. "They may be perceived as experts when they are not," Nieves said, "or they may be seen as the person closest to the issue when, in fact, they may be removed from the issue and have to go consult other community leaders."

However, those quoted by the media, especially those in power, would be amenable to suggestions by the media if they offered solutions or revealed pertinent new facts. But Chicago Hispanic media rarely provide something more than simplistic information. Said Jauregui: "You will find a certain resistance to controversial ideas at the top.

They have not reached the level of independence, so they can afford to treat issues as they should be treated."

This meek, sporadic tilting at windmills angers some readers who believe it is incumbent on Spanish-language media to crusade for Hispanic rights, particularly when these aren't recognized by mainstream media. Businesswoman Anita Villarreal, head of the Little Village Chamber of Commerce, has urged Hispanic media to do more than regurgitate a spokesman's words.

"They have the power," she said. "It's there, but it's not being used. They're very active in social events and they can get lots of people to come out to them. That's because they can sell the event to a sponsor. But it takes more than that to fulfill the role."

The Problems

Newspapers were, by far, the medium to receive the harshest criticism. "The print medium is awful, quite awful," Adler said. "In every sense. Written very badly, hardly any original reporting, sell their space to the highest bidder, print verbatim any press release."

Said Nieves: "The black community has the Chicago Defender and it's read by everyone and you can get it at any newsstand. You don't see that with any of our papers. The closest is La Raza and it's not there yet. We can get there, but we still have a long way to go."

Luis Rossi, publisher of the weekly La Raza, defends his newspaper's quality. He said it has been improving steadily as resources become available. "As we progress and make money, we get better," Rossi said. "I think we have improved tremendously from years past."

Newspapers, however, weren't the only ones sharply criticized. The Latino Committee on the Media (LCOM), a group of Hispanic professionals who monitor both English- and Spanish-language mass media, reports that improvements in press and broadcast outlets are made only under pressure -- from the community or the competition.

"There really is no concern for quality," said founder Mary Gonzalez Koenig. "The idea is the bottom line. And it's not that they don't have money. They do. The sales are there."

Some of the criticisms sounded familiar. After all, any media outlet just starting off could easily fall victim to such censure. However, the activists expressed a concern that media managements feel no need to improve as long as budgets are met and advertisers found.

Other grievances include:

* The quality of reporting is dismal. There is a lack of seasoned reporters covering important issues, and those who have been around are lured away by the Anglo media with better pay and working conditions.

"There is a lot of one-sided reporting," said Jauregui. "The reporters do not question the answers they get and if the answers are wrong what happens is that the community is misinformed. They're constantly being manipulated by the interviewee."

David Cordova, news director at Telemundo's Channel 44, said his two reporters are always pressed for time. "Our quality has improved," Cordova said, "but we have limited resources. We don't have any luxuries. To a certain point I agree there's a problem in covering news profoundly."

* Management is not willing to spend the money to increase news staffs. Deborah Folga, former general manager of WTAQ and a member of LCOM, said that since about 1986 the three Spanish-language radio stations have been reducing staff. She said she was often told not to make a move unless it would result in profit.

"I needed to get extra help for election coverage and I was told to send the sales staff. You just couldn't get the funds," she said.

Luis de Gonzalez, news director for the AM/FM combo WOJO/WIND, said the two stations' news staffs were consolidated when Tichenor, which already owned WIND, bought WOJO. "Some positions were eliminated because there was duplication. But it doesn't mean that quality has suffered," he said.

The problem, he added, arises because "every little organization wants us to send one reporter to a function. We can't. We have to use them for the events we consider newsworthy."

The Tichenor stations have six full-time news staffers as well as several correspondents.

* Conflicts of interest are an acceptable way of doing business. If an advertiser makes some type of controversial news, media look the other way. In one case, a car wash owner was arrested on drug charges. He was later shot in his bedroom. Neither event ever made it on the air because his company advertised with the media.

"They were more interested in cultivating clients," said Edward Villarreal, former news director of Channel 44. "Their concern was whether a client was going to open a store or have a cocktail party, not the economics or politics of the city."

Cordova counters that the station maintains a strict code of ethics. "We try very hard to be impartial and present both sides," he said.

* **There are no analytical or investigative pieces.** Activists called this "announcement journalism" or "bulletin board journalism." The media -- newspapers in particular -- often run such items word-for-word, without editing.

"There's no vision," lamented Nieves. "It's a knee-jerk reaction to the issues. I suppose that is because this is a new game for us."

Part of the problem, says Channel 44's Cordova, is that Spanish-language media are constantly losing their good reporters once they get enough experience to provide depth. "We're the farm system and they're the major leagues. In the non-Hispanic market, the salaries are better," he said.

* **Media owners and managerss have a misperception of the community that can result in condescending and patronizing programming.** Folga calls it a "ghettoizing mentality."

Said Koenig: "It's not what is going to be best for the community, but what is going to be best for the old bottom line. And that's okay because the media are businesses. But sometimes you have to take a look at the quality and how well you're serving the constituency.

"Compare them to the black-owned (stations). They're heavily into issues and information, input, output from the community. Spanish media do not give that to the community. They do what they have to and no more. They think the consumer doesn't know better."

IX. The Future

To predict is to invite inaccuracy, for no one can look into the future or use the past to define with certainty what is ahead. However, trends and tendencies of the Spanish-language media market help one to assume -- with a degree of safety -- that some things will happen if newspapers, radio, and television stations continue the track record of yesteryear. This forecast, like one about the weather, may be true in certain regions of the country but entirely off base in others. If there is one constant in the field of U.S. Hispanic media, it is that they are flexible, continuously redefining their roles and paths as circumstances require.

One thing can be stated with certainty. The death knell sounded by those within and without the industry a decade or two ago has proved false. What's more, many Spanish-language media outlets are thriving despite increased competition. One can write with confidence that this generation will not see the wilting away of these media as long as they continue to improve and adjust. Beyond that, projections must be couched with care. Much will depend on immigration. Spanish-language media will survive as long as Latin Americans continue to pour into this country fleeing economic deprivations and political upheaval. Much will also depend on retention of language. If U.S. Latinos speak, read, and write Spanish after the third and fourth generations, they will look for media that serve them in a way mainstream media do not. Finally, survival will depend, too, on how well Spanish-language media serve their audience _vis_ _a_ _vis_ mainstream media targeting Hispanics.

The audience is what gives media power. Without those listeners and readers, a newspaper or broadcast outlet would be like the proverbial tree that falls in the forest with no one to hear it. As the influence of that audience within the mainstream grows, so too will the influence of its print and broadcast media -- if they are the media of choice. What occurs now is not that Latinos do not use the Spanish-language media; it is that Latinos who make up the predominant audience of these media tend to be the recent arrivals, the Spanish-dependent, the disenfranchised underclass. And while Spanish-language media must not lose sight of their responsibilities (and advocacy role) to this group, they cannot afford to continue losing the more assimilated bilingual Hispanic -- if they ever had him.

The swelling ranks of Latinos in this country are already a force to be reckoned with, whether they have voting power or not. Yet it is only the dedicated public official, or one of their own, who will consider their concerns without a wary eye on election time. Nonetheless, the rise of Latino politicians on the national scene as well as the growing clout of soon-to-be voters can mean a concurrent increase in the influence of their media -- if those media truly count these voters as their audience. Language, thus, will not be as much of a stumbling block as in the past because more people in power will understand Spanish and those who don't will have aides who do.

At the same time, however, language will remain a dividing line. Not a barrier or a wall, but a crease in the immense quilt that is Hispanic America. Two distinct media markets -- separate but not necessarily equal, with some common bonds -- will emerge: the bilingual or English-dominant Hispanic and the Spanish-dependent. Often the two will be divided along generational lines. We see this happening already. Second- and third-generation Latinos may watch NBC. Their parents or newly arrived aunts prefer Univision. (In some cases, Latinos watch both.) Language, to a certain extent, already determines content, with the Spanish-language media usually concentrating on Latin American news. The crossover by bilingual Hispanics to Spanish media _may_ occur if and when the media cover issues that relate to Hispanics in the United States as well as those across the border. Yes, bilingual Latinos are concerned about Latin America, but the issues that affect their daily lives are more important: the public transportation strike, the lifting of controlled rents, immigration law changes, the 1990 Census. Beyond the news, social matters of _el barrio_ must also be addressed: changing values within the family, single parenting, nursing home care for the elderly.

What else can we expect in the future?

* There will emerge more Spanish-language national magazines targeted for an increasingly segmented market. This will make the Hispanic print market more attractive to advertisers because, like radio, these magazines will reach a specific, well-defined market. We will also see more English-language, Hispanic-oriented publications. Already in stands or on the drawing board are: _Hispanic_, _Que Pasa_, _Latin Beat_, and Univision's projected magazine in Spanish.

Some believe that the entry of these publications into the market will bring in more ad dollars. But others, such as Zeke Montes, a publisher and past president of the National Association of Hispanic Publications, says the same ad revenue pie is being divided into more pieces. While there is definitely a niche for both English- and Spanish-language publications, their success will be determined by how well they have identified that niche, how accessible that niche is, and how well they perform their role. Hispanic Business, for instance, does a remarkable job with what it intends to do -- and it is successful.

These magazines may be influential if they have a vast market -- such as the Univision magazine is expected to have -- or if they reach a select, powerful, albeit small audience of grassroots leaders and opinion molders.

* **Print and broadcast media will expand and improve their verification and auditing of media audiences.** Spanish-language newspapers, radio, and television stations can no longer sit back and complain about undercounting and expect advertisers to buy them as a token gesture. The lack of hard numbers, inflated figures, and widespread complaints about audience measurements have slowed progress. At the time of this writing, the National Association of Hispanic Publications was offering its members the chance to be part of a "group buy" provided they got their circulation audited.

Though Spanish-language radio stations are narrowing their audiences as more stations divide the market into smaller but more definable groups, there are still problems with unreliable radio measurements. Embarassingly wide gaps among the figures of the audience-measurement services -- Arbitron, Strategy Research, and Birch -- certainly dampen the enthusiasm of any advertiser. It will be to radio's benefit to establish some method amenable to broadcasters, ad agencies, and measurement services alike. Perhaps a combination of the phone method with the more expensive door-to-door method will help, or special Hispanic reports based on a six-month sample rather than three.

Television has made the most progress. In a commendable effort by both Telemundo and Univision, the two Spanish-language networks joined forces to set up a national ratings method employing "people meter" households. It is to be tested in Los Angeles before going national.

* **There will be more consolidation both within a medium and among different media.** Maybe an Anglo or Latino owner with an existing Spanish-language newspaper -- or radio station -- will attempt to buy other dailies or weeklies in the country to form a chain a la Gannett or Knight-Ridder. Because of the enormous cost and leverage power needed for such acquisitions, look for an established company to show interest in this.

Networks will continue to purchase stations to the maximum allowed by law, then turn to another medium -- print or radio -- for expansion. Univision, for instance, was planning a magazine at the time of this writing. A radio station or two in the top Hispanic markets may also be a likely acquisition for this company.

This will mean that the ability to influence will rest in the hands of the few, not the many -- a situation not unlike the English-language media. The power of any large network-type operation to mobilize people, create leaders, and affect government policy will increase because there will be more ways to present the same idea -- by print, radio, and television -- at various times, in different ways, and in many communities.

* **More diversified and quality programming in television will come about as a result of audience demand.** Though novelas still make up the bulk of programming, there has been a gradual movement to include other types of shows -- some domestically produced -- in the television lineup.

With the entry of Hallmark and the Reliance Group, the audience has seen the addition of Univision's "Portada" and Telemundo's "Dia a Dia" among a variety of other cooking, music/variety, and special documentary shows. Sitcoms have been added, too, but they are non-U.S. produced and will probably continue to be imported because of their high cost of production.

Though ECO, the all-news-and-information cable operation, offers an alternative to the two networks for information, it originates in Mexico and has few substantial clips and programs from the United States.

* **Television networks will eventually emerge as the medium that can transcend regional and cultural differences among the different Hispanic groups.** Spanish-language television's development parallels that of its English-language counterpart. Spanish TV today is the English TV of the '50s and early '60s -- growing, fumbling, and progressing. It still has a long way to go, but the potential is there, if the power to inform and influence is used well.

This potential to transcend differences may prove to be the most important factor in the influence equation on a national level. U.S. Hispanics are a heterogeneous group that has long been divided regionally, politically, and socially. While most Latinos tend to favor bilingual education and reject English-only initiatives,(1) there are some distinct variations in political affiliations. Mexican-Americans and Puerto Ricans, for example, are overwhelmingly Democrat. Cubans, on the other hand, tend to be Republican. Television network programming can highlight the commonalities of the various groups, without ignoring or belittling the differences. Radio and newspapers, by the nature of their formats, tend to be too local.

* **The trend in Anglo ownership of Hispanic media will continue.** A growing interest in the market means big companies will take on smaller media and ad firms. Though this means an infusion of money for programming and from advertisers, it also signals a loss of power for the Hispanic community and a silent resentment among the audience.

Many leaders interviewed for this book doubted the commitment of non-Hispanic owners to the Latino audience.

"It's the Rent-a-Mexican syndrome," said Raquel Oliva, a San Antonio businesswoman and community activist. "If we were the owners, we could become more influential, and we would be more sensitive to the issues of Hispanics."

Consequences are steep if Spanish-language media, content to rest on their laurels, resist change and improvement. Already English-language media managers, realizing the potential of and profit in the market, have gone after Latino readers, viewers, and listeners full force. Newsday in New York, the Los Angeles Times' bilingual supplement Nuestro Tiempo, and television stations in Miami are prime examples of an aggressive attempt to attract Hispanics with better coverage and more Hispanic reporters. It can be hoped that groups like the Latino Committee on the Media in Chicago and the Hispanic Media Coalition in Los Angeles will spring up in the major Hispanic markets to keep tabs on progress and to force change in both Latino and Anglo media.

To ensure quality, Spanish-language media will have to:

* **Develop a cadre of reporters, train them, and pay them well.** For too long, Spanish-language media have either imported talent from Latin America or served as a farm system for the English-language stations and newspapers in their area. This has left them with staffs who do not always speak English well, do not understand local issues, and lack perspective on events in the community.

* **Invest money in their public affairs and news programming.** There should be more documentary pieces, more investigative stories, more explanatory journalism. Covering a press conference is not enough; neither is rewriting a press release. Sending the sales staff out to cover the local elections is not acceptable, either.

* **Overcome infighting among sectors within the media.** Published news reports and leaders interviewed expressed a growing concern that Hispanics of Mexican descent are losing their voice in Spanish-language media, particularly in television. References were made to "Easternization" and "Cubanization" of the outlets. They pointed mainly to Univision, which has plans to consolidate production operations in Miami, features Cuban-American show hosts, and lacks Mexican-American representation in top management. Univision has denied this. Whether perception or reality, this concern is a stumbling block to the progress of Spanish-language media.

These media would do well to heed the warnings. "As we go forward as a community, we will learn to use our presence," said Guillermo Linares, an educator and activist in New York's Dominican community. "The media will have to place themselves in a position to be more responsive to our needs. They will have no choice in the matter if they want to survive."

Notes

Introduction

[1] Clint C. Wilson II and Felix Gutierrez, *Minorities and Media: Diversity and the End of Mass Communication* (Beverly Hills: Sage Publications, 1985), p. 193.

Chapter I

[1] Articles in the press have also been critical of Telemundo's news programming. Juan Carlos Cotto, "Spanish News Gives CNN Ratings Lesson," *Miami Herald*, July 9, 1989, p. 1K.

[2] Janet L. Therrien, Katz Hispanic Radio Research, Winter 1989 data.

[3] Janet L. Therrien, "A Comparison of Strategy Research, Arbitron and Birch Hispanic Audience Measurements in New York" (Katz Hispanic Radio Research, Fall 1987).

Chapter II

[1] U.S. Department of Commerce, Bureau of the Census, *Hispanic Population in the United States: March 1988* (Current Population Reports Series P-20, No. 431, Aug. 1988).

[2] *Ibid.*, p. 1.

[3] *Ibid.*, p. 4.

[4] *Ibid.*, p. 4.

[5] *Ibid.*, p. 4.

[6] Teresa Menendez, Conversations and a letter dated Oct. 6, 1989. Focus group sessions conducted in Los Angeles, New York, Miami, San Antonio.

[7] Yankelovich, Skelly & White, Inc., *Spanish USA: A Study of the Hispanic Market in the United States* (a report to the SIN National Television Network), 1981.
See also, 1984 edition of this study.

[8] Calvin Veltman, *The Future of the Spanish Language in the United States* (Washington, D.C.: Hispanic Policy Development Project, 1988), p. 66.

[9] Kim, Y.Y., "Toward an Interactive Theory of Communication - Acculturation" *Communication Yearbook 3, 1979* pp. 436-453.
See also, Pamela J. Shoemaker, Stephen D. Reese, and Wayne A. Danielson, "Media in Ethnic Context," University of Texas at Austin, College of Communication, Nov. 1985, p. 27.

[10] Harry P. Pachon and Louis DeSipio, *The Latino Vote in 1988* (Washington, D.C.: National Association of Latino Elected and Appointed Officials Education Fund, 1988), p. 8.

[11] *Ibid.*, p. 10.

[12] *Ibid.*, p. 13.

[13] *Ibid.*, p. 13.

[14] *Ibid.*, p. 2.

[15] *Ibid.*, p. 7.

[16] Strategy Research Corp., *1989 U.S. Hispanic Market* (Miami: Strategy Research Corp., 1989), pp. 337-360.

Chapter III

[1] Ray Eldon Hiebert, Donald F. Ungurait, and Thomas W. Bohn, *Mass Media: Introduction to Mass Communication* (New York: David McKay Company, Inc., 1974), p. 5.

[2] Fernando Ferrer, "The Report of the Hunts Point Task Force, January 1989," Bronx, New York.

[3] Bernard Berelson, "Communications and Public Opinion," Mass Communications, Wilbur Schramm, ed., (Urbana: University of Illinois Press, 1949), p. 500.

[4] Pamela J. Shoemaker, Stephen D. Reese, and Wayne A. Danielson, "Media in Ethnic Context," University of Texas at Austin, College of Communication, Nov. 1985, p. 35.

[5] Victor Valle, "Ethnic Fight Heats Up at Latino Station," Los Angeles Times, May 19, 1989, Part IV, p. 1.
Also, Seth Mydans, "Charges of Bias in Spanish-Language Television," New York Times, July 23, 1989.

Chapter IV

[1] Strategy Research Corp., 1989 U.S. Hispanic Market, pp. 115-120.

Chapter V

[1] Strategy Research Corp., 1989 U.S. Hispanic Market, pp. 122-128.

Chapter VI

[1] Strategy Research Corp., 1989 U.S. Hispanic Market, pp. 130-134.

[2] Carlos Harrison, "Region Becoming More Latin, but Less Cuban," Miami Herald, Sept. 12, 1988, p. 1B.

Chapter VII

[1] Strategy Research Corp., 1989 U.S. Hispanic Market, pp. 136-142.

Chapter VIII

[1] Strategy Research Corp., 1989 U.S. Hispanic Market, pp. 150-155.

Chapter IX

[1] Federico Subervi, "The Democratic and Republican Parties' Latino-Oriented Mass Communication Strategies During the 1988 Elections," University of Texas at Austin, Department of Radio-Television-Film, 1989, p. 3.

Ana Veciana-Suarez

Ana Veciana-Suarez is a general-assignment writer for the Palm Beach Post. She has been a journalist since 1978, starting her career with the Miami News before moving to the Miami Herald organization in 1982. She joined the Palm Beach Post in 1988. She holds a degree in mass communications from the University of South Florida, where she graduated summa cum laude. Ms. Veciana-Suarez has received several awards, including the Clarion Award for human-rights reporting from Women in Communications, and awards from the Society of Professional Journalists. She is the author of Hispanic Media, USA, also published by The Media Institute.

The Media Institute

The Media Institute is a nonprofit, tax-exempt research foundation supported by a wide range of foundations, corporations, associations, and individuals. From its headquarters in Washington, D.C., the Institute sponsors various programs related to communications policy, business/media relations, the new technologies, and First Amendment issues.

The work of The Media Institute is made possible through the generosity of its financial supporters. To make a tax-deductible gift, or for more information, please contact Patrick D. Maines, President, at the address below.

Editor: Richard T. Kaplar
Production: David P. Taggart

the media institute

3017 M Street, N.W.
Washington, D.C. 20007
202-298-7512

P94.5.H58 V429 1990

P94.5.H58 V429 1990